The Voice of the Shepherdess

Edited By
Peter J. McCord

With an Introduction by
Anne Llewellyn Barstow

Sheed & Ward
Kansas City

Sheed & Ward™ is a service of The National Catholic Reporter Publishing Company.

Library of Congress Cataloguing-in-Publication Data

The voice of the shepherdess / edited by Peter J. McCord : with
  introduction by Anne Llewellyn Barstow.
      p.   cm.
   Includes bibliographical references.
   ISBN 1-55612-819-3 (alk. paper)
   1. Ordination of women—Catholic Church.   2. Women clergy.
3. Catholic Church—Clergy.   I. McCord, Peter J.
BX1912.2.V64 1996
262'.142'082—dc20   96-6982
                                                                              CIP

Published by: Sheed & Ward
               115 E. Armour Blvd.
               P.O. Box 419492
               Kansas City, MO 64141-6492

To order, call: (800) 333-7373

Cover photograph of Rev. Janet Vincent-Scaringe by Roger Bonsteel.

Cover design by James F. Brisson.

This book is dedicated to the women who have been the key inspiration and support of my life: Mary, the mother of Jesus, Mary, my own mother; Mary-Lou, my sister; Honey, my adopted sister; Barbara, my sister-in-law; and Ann Elizabeth, my loving wife of thirty years. It is also dedicated to the women who have sought in the past, are now seeking and will strive in the future to serve the Lord Jesus in faithfulness to His call upon their lives.

"There does not exist among you Jew or Greek, slave or freeman, male or female. All are one in Christ Jesus."

— Galatians 3:28.

"It is He Who is our peace, and Who made the two of us one by breaking down the barrier of hostility that kept us apart."

— Ephesians 2:14.

"Surely we cannot help speaking of what we have heard and seen."

— Acts 4:20.

Contents

Editor's Preface

Peter J. McCord

Why this book? Are there not already available a large number of books on feminist theology? And haven't a number of books already been published indicating women's attitudes toward ministerial roles? The answer, of course, is "yes." But, in reviewing the literature at the time this book was conceived in mid-1994, it seemed there was a lack of real life experience included. There was theory, whether theological, philosophical, social, psychological or whatever. There was opinion, both as to the origins of the present situation and the predictability of changes or lack of them in the future. What was lacking at the time, however, was the story element: what is actually happening in the churches, in the lived experience of women in ministry? More recently, a book was published, telling the stories of a group of ten female pastors serving one denomination's churches within a particular geographical area (*Women Pastors.* New York: Crossroad Publishing Co., 1995).

Within my own Christian family (Roman Catholic), there has been an abundance of literature on the subject and even strong organizations formed, such as the Women's Ordination Conference and Priests for Equality, to bring about change. This process of advancing women's ministerial roles in our tradition was abruptly halted, though not surprisingly, when Pope John Paul II issued a letter to the Catholic bishops on May 22, 1994, declaring that ". . . the church has no authority whatsoever to confer priestly ordination on women and . . . this judgment is to be definitively held by all the church's faithful." In other words, it is not to be the subject of discussion or debate in official Catholic circles or publications anymore. Any doubts about the seriousness of the Pope's conviction on this matter should have been resolved by the publication, on November 18, 1995, of the papally-approved *Responsum ad dubium* from the Congregation of the Faith, confirming that the papal teaching on the inadmissibility of women to ordination does, in fact, belong to the deposit of faith, i.e. is infallible teaching.

Given the consistent affirmation from Pope John Paul II (following Pope Paul VI) that the ordination of women is precluded by the *very nature of the church*, a second problem arises. In a time when strong ecumenical initiatives have been and still are being pursued among many Christian denominations, the position on women in ministry becomes an ecumenical, as well as a doctrinal point of departure. Almost twenty years ago, I was privileged to edit a book on the ecumenical problem presented by the papacy (*A Pope for All Christians?*, New York: Paulist Press, 1976), to which seven theologians from different traditions contributed. All but one of them, much to my surprise, affirmed that there was indeed a role for a leader representing the entire Christian family, though significant modifications would have to be made to achieve unity on this subject. In other words, the *concept* of the papacy was not so much of an ecumenical problem as the actual *practice* of the papal role.

In the case of women's ministerial roles, however, the case has been stated as *constitutive of the very nature* of Christian community. In this position, there is no room for compromise of any sort. If, in this scenario, effective unity within the Christian family were to be achieved at some later date, it could only happen, in the Pope's view, by an agreement among all the Christian churches who currently ordain women to pastoral roles, to "decommission" their women ministers, repent of their error, and return to the "one fold and one shepherd." Given the apparent irreversibility of the process of women sharing roles traditionally held exclusively by men, the prospects of an ecumenical accommodation along these lines seems to be virtually nonexistent. Thus the subject of women, in ecumenical terms, has become a "stone of contradiction," dividing the Christian family.

What to do? Among the many Christian denominations who ordain women ministers, there has been disappointment, though not surprise, at the papal position. It is perceived as another wedge, among others, preventing effective unity and understanding between the churches from occurring. Among some evangelical churches, for example the Southern Baptist, it would be a point of agreement with the Pope, though they do not recognize his authority to make this pronouncement – they simply concur that is "scriptural." Among

Catholics, there has been anger, dismay, wholehearted agreement, simple or grudging acceptance or indifference.

It is the purpose of this book to confront the issue head-on from an *ecumenical* perspective. In John 17:21, Jesus prays ". . . that all may be one as you, Father, are in me, and I in you: I pray that they may be one in us, that the world may believe that you sent me." This text is also the theme of Pope John Paul II's recent encyclical on church unity and the role of Peter, *Ut Unum Sint,* published on May 25, 1995. This book, then, is based on the premise that the overall credibility of the Gospel is called into question, if the churches cannot agree on this very vital and fundamental question – a point reemphasized, I might add, in the Pope's *Letter to Women* dated June 29, 1995.

The form of this book, however, is not polemical. Rather than primarily discussing theory, *The Voice of the Shepherdess* is based on the stories of eight women who are actually engaged in pastoral ministry in eight different Christian traditions. For example, the Catholic participant, though not ordained, is a licensed Catholic Chaplain in a Catholic hospital and engaged in a ministry tradition-ally performed exclusively by men. These women present a diversity which is geographical as well as denominational. What they have in common is a recognized ministry in a Christian faith tradition, fulfilling roles formerly held by men exclusively. It was my convic-tion that the lived experience, the individual stories of these women, would speak more powerfully about how the Spirit is actually work-ing in the churches than any of the usual arguments from tradition or scriptural interpretation. It was the proclamation of the Good News of Jesus Christ, the *story* of Jesus, that convicted the hearts of early converts to Christianity, and still does today. The reader can judge whether these stories are Good News or not, whether the Spirit is indeed working in their lives or they, and many others, are simply victims of a tragic deception or misguided zeal.

Each participant was asked, in the course of telling her story, to address five questions:

- How did you personally hear and respond to the call to enter into pastoral ministry?
- What was the response to your decision among your peers and those responsible for your training and formation as a minister?
- How has it worked out for you in actual practice, i.e., do those you serve accept and apparently benefit from your ministry? Evi-dences of this?

- What do you see in the foreseeable future, in terms of the opportunities for women to serve in pastoral roles previously assigned
  exclusively to men?
- How do you view the firm position of the Roman Catholic and
  some other Christian churches regarding the exclusion of women
  from ordained pastoral ministry in ecumenical terms, i.e., as an
  obstacle to understanding and reconciliation among Christian
  churches?

The book provides a forum, often unavailable in institutional
settings, for women to speak on their own terms and in their own
words, based on their own experience. Perhaps it is a testimony to
their longing to have a voice that everyone asked to contribute to
the book agreed to do so, with very little persuasion. It is my hope
that *The Voice of the Shepherdess* will be heard with compassion,
understanding, discernment and love.

Because I felt that these accounts by women pastors would
benefit from seeing them within a wider historical context, I asked
Anne Llewellyn Barstow to write an introduction. I had been struck
by both her scholarly research and compassionate concern for
women's issues while doing background research for this book. The
reader is invited to share this wealth of knowledge by consulting her
work: *Joan of Arc: Heretic, Mystic, Shaman* (Lewiston: Ed. Mellen
Press, 1986), *Witchcraze, A New History of the European Witch Hunts*
(San Francisco: Pandora, A Div. of Harper Collins Publishers, 1994),
Married Priests and the Reforming Papacy (Lewiston: Ed. Mellen Press,
1982).

I am particularly grateful, not only to the women whose stories
we read here, who may have taken some measure of risk by having
their experiences and thoughts appear in print, but also to those who
gave me their names, since I knew none of them when the book was
conceived.

So my grateful appreciation goes to Ms. Elizabeth Congdon,
Rev. John Haughey, S.J., Pastor John Rush, Rev. Ken Owens, Rev.
Joseph A. Burgess, Rev. Kent Allen and Rev. Ed McLeod. I am also
grateful to Rev. Ann Davis and Rev. Elizabeth Layman, whose
experiences originally inspired me to think about doing this book.

Peter J. McCord
Taylors, South Carolina
December 25, 1995

Introduction

Anne Llewellyn Barstow

"Women must turn to one another for stories, they must share the stories of their lives and their hopes and their unacceptable fantasies."
                    – Carolyn Heilbrun, *Writing a Woman's Life*

The entry of women into the ordained clergy provides as deep a spiritual struggle for the churches as any issue of our time. At one level it challenges the image of the religious leader as exclusively defined by male gender, with all of the privileges of leadership – dispensing the sacraments, formulating ideas, controlling money and property – reserved to men. On a deeper level, it opens the very nature of Christian spirituality to being enriched more fully by women's experience. From their position on the fringe of the churches women have always contributed to religious life, but now, as preachers, officiants and theologians, they are adding their spiritual insight to the fundamental structure of Christianity.

This extraordinary step in the ongoing history of the churches is welcomed by some, feared and resisted by others. Let us look at the experience of the Episcopal Church in the United States as an example.

Before 1970 there had been little serious discussion in the Episcopal Church about ordaining women. However, as the women's movement began to stir discussion about whether the Gospel should be applied differently to women than men, women began entering seminaries to prepare themselves for sharing in ordained ministry. At its General Convention in 1970, the Church voted to ordain women as deacons; a similar move for ordination to priesthood was narrowly defeated.

At the next triennial convention, in 1973, a large number of women presented themselves as fully qualified candidates for priesthood. But a conservative reaction had set in and the resolution was defeated again. The women's feeling of betrayal ran deep. A group of eleven determined women decided to be ordained without canonical approval. Declaring that their "primary motive is to begin to free priesthood from the bondage it suffers as long as it is characterized by categorical exclusion of persons on the basis of sex,"[1] they reaffirmed that male gender was not necessary for ordination. Three bishops agreed to perform the ceremony, which was held in Philadelphia in July 1974. This act plunged the Episcopal Church into a crisis which was still raging when the next General Convention met in 1976. After a long debate and five minutes of silent prayer, the ordination of women was approved by a strong vote. The life of the Episcopal Church was changed forever in that moment.

As other churches have found as they have taken the same road, the way is not easy. A small number of priests and congregations (less than half of 1% of the Church) left the Episcopal Church over the issue of women priests and related matters. In leaving they expressed two beliefs harmful to women:

> that priests must bear a physical resemblance to Christ (i.e., must have male bodies) and that women lack the character and intellect to be priests. The first reason was used by Pope John Paul II in 1994 when he reiterated that women cannot be ordained in the Roman Catholic Church.

The second reason also has a very long history. Although in the Gospels Jesus is not pictured as denigrating women, the Pauline letters give a mixed message. By the time the Constantinian Church was established, the Church Fathers were writing about the "weakness" and even the "evil" of women's nature, which disqualified them for ordination. These pernicious ideas were repeated in the theology of the Church and fed to the faithful in sermons until they built a foundation of Christian misogyny capable of causing women great harm. The burning of women as "witches" in the sixteenth and seventeenth centuries, carried out in the name of the churches, could not have occurred without that basis of woman-hating in Christian doctrine.[2]

Some Episcopalian congregants and clergy have refused to accept the Eucharist from a woman priest, sometimes causing a scandalous disruption of the sacrament. In one case, a male priest reached across the altar rail and tried to grab the chalice from the Rev. Carter Heyward, who was officiating. As the Rev. Heyward struggled to hold on to it, he clawed her hands until they bled, saying, "May you burn in hell."

After twenty years of bitter debate, in 1994 the Church of England (Anglican) ordained its first women priests. When this happened, a rector in Lincolnshire expressed his fury by comparing women priests to "witches and dogs."[3] There is more than a power struggle between the sexes involved in the words of these men: they reveal the hatred of women that centuries of unchallenged Christian misogyny can produce.

But these, fortunately, are isolated events. A continuing problem has been the more subtle resistance of refusing to hire women as rectors, relegating them to assistants' jobs. At the level of national staffs and seminary faculties, women remain a small minority. Still, in nineteen years, women priests have gained wide acceptance. Numbering about a thousand, they are beginning to change both the image of priesthood and the theology of the Church by ministering out of their female experience.

The first clergywoman in the United States was ordained by the Congregational Church in 1853, but it was many years before Congregationalists or others began to ordain women in numbers.[4] Spiritual searching and political action have reinforced each other in this movement. For example, the spiritual equality of men and women upheld by Quakers inspired much of the first Women's Movement that began in the 1850s, while the victory of suffrage for women in 1920 helped women in the Methodist Church to gain ordination soon after. Since that time, all of the mainline Protestant churches have taken the same step, except for the Missouri Synod Lutherans and the Southern Baptist Convention. Individual Southern Baptist churches, however, may ordain whomever they choose; some have ordained women, but the issue remains controversial.

Pentecostal churches, true to their belief in the power of the Holy Spirit to move where it will, have ordained women for years, producing many powerful women preachers in both black and white churches. But a number of other evangelical churches and the Roman Catholic and Orthodox churches do not ordain women. The Pope, in fact, has forbidden Catholics to discuss the issue.

Meanwhile, the thousands of women who serve as ministers and priests, in cooperation with their congregations, are forging a new experience of church. It is precisely that female experience that

this book is about. As seven Protestant clergywomen and one lay
Catholic hospital chaplain reflect on their ministries, they lament
the obstacles they still face because of their gender while celebrating
the opportunities for serving Christ that are newly theirs. Their
stories are moving and inspiring. They are also remarkable for their
modesty and humility. Perhaps these women are still too deeply
immersed in being women ministers to realize how much their
witness means to their churches. Their work is the essential part of
a historical growth process in North American Christianity that is
blossoming at the end of the twentieth century.

There is much here that testifies to how painful such growth
always is. Some of the women have been stereotyped by ordination
committees, ignored by placement committees, and mistaken by
parishioners for the receptionist or for the minister's wife. Their call
to ordination has been assumed to be less important to them than
their call to be a wife. Their ideas have been ignored by male
colleagues, their sermons rewritten or even walked out on. Church
members have refused to accept counseling with them, and have even
refused to accept Communion from them. They have learned that
to succeed they must work twice as hard as a man.

Perhaps even more troubling than these rebuffs are the questions of image which several women raise. Ministers are traditionally
expected to be figures of authority, assertive and, in some cases,
authoritarian. Yet none of these women want to minister in that
way; they struggle between this role expectation and their desire to
work in partnership with their congregations. This problem remains
acute for some of these writers. As one woman confessed, "I learned
to accept that I was unacceptable."

The lay Catholic chaplain presents still another problem: what
happens in ecumenical work when all of the ministers except the
Catholic one are ordained, a problem she frequently faces. As she
preaches, conducts funerals, and carries out an interdenominational
ministry at her hospital, she constantly encounters public situations
in which people don't know how to respond to her and she isn't
sure what she should do.

But all of these difficulties, major and minor, pale beside the
positive values of being female ministers. Their very gender is an
advantage in many ways. Almost all witness to the importance of
traditional female traits for doing ministry: what they learned about
nurturing from raising children; the importance of community, of
sharing leadership and carrying out co-ministry; the ability to listen,

to negotiate, to sympathize. While these are traits which men can learn, they are taught to most women from the beginning of their lives.

Some of the writers speak more directly about the importance of femaleness. Two witness to the powerful influence of their grandmothers' faith. Another writes about the image of minister as mother, and the power of preaching during Advent when she was herself pregnant. One reports that a female parishioner could tell her things that she could not say to male clergy. And another notes how children's expectations of who can be a minister expanded when she became their pastor.

These accounts describe women's ministry at the daily level of parish life. The further struggle to incorporate women's experience into theology and liturgy is scarcely launched. It needs the support of all men and women. One of the major attempts to further that work, the Reimagining Conference of 1994 in Minneapolis, an interdenominational gathering of international scope, invited women to imagine some of the feminine aspects of the sacred. Despite its Biblical basis, it was strongly attacked by conservatives. The top woman in the Presbyterian Church was fired and a virtual witchhunt was carried out in the Presbyterian and Methodist denominations. The conference is referred to in one of the articles here as promoting heresy. Yet many of the women who attended the conference found it to be a moment of great spiritual empowerment. We have to remember that "women" does not signify a monolithic category and that different women have different spiritual needs.

Through all of the accounts in this book runs the power of the Holy Spirit, or what some of the writers choose to call Grace, which sought them out, often to their surprise, and led them down the difficult but amazing path to ordination. If anyone should wonder "Why have women pastors?" the answer surely is here: that God calls women as well as men to clerical leadership, and that women respond in these authentic ways.

NOTES

1. Mary S. Donovan, *Women Priests in the Episcopal Church: The Experience Of the First Decade.* Forward Movement Publications, 1988.
2. See Anne L. Barstow, *Witchcraze: A New History of the European Witch Hunts.* (Harper, 1994) Thousands of women were put to death on the charge of being servants of the Devil, of worshipping him, having sex with him, and carrying out his plans for the destruction of Christian society.

3. *New York Times,* I.1.5 (March 13, 1994).

4. For an account of the new paths in ministry being forged by Congregational (United Church of Christ) women ministers, see The Berkshire
Clergywomen and Allison Stokes, *Women Pastors* (Crossroad, 1995).

1

Called by Grace

Chaplain Bryna Bozart

It is curious, now that I think about it. I never had a thought to enter the ministry. In the beginning, I would not have understood that concept. The idea would have been alien to me. I imagine I would have responded very much like Mary's query. How? Mary had wondered how she was to become the mother of Jesus and I would have wondered how I could assume a man's role. As a girl-child born into traditions and culture unfriendly to the notion of women ministers, I would have had no way then of envisioning who I am today.

How did I hear God's call to ministry? How did it all really happen?

My story must begin with the early influences I remember as significant. I was born into a Protestant, Southern tradition and culture. It wasn't until I was nine years old that my parents converted to Catholicism, and I, too, became a Catholic. My first memories of God and the things of God center around my maternal grandmother. She lived out in the country, at the base of Lookout Mountain in Georgia, when I came into her life. I would spend part of each summer in childhood with her. She told me stories from the Bible and sang to me snatches of old hymns. She spoke to me of Jesus and softly sang of "Amazing Grace," "Just a Closer Walk with Thee" and beautifully haunting phrases of "In the Garden."

We sat on her front porch, the head of her bird dog nestled on my lap. The sounds of the night surrounded us in the glow of the moonlight. I watched lightning bugs floating like stars in that summer air, wondering where they went when daylight broke. I wondered, too, where would I go when I grew up? Would I have a glow and if so, where would my light shine?

Another person who greatly influenced me in childhood was my paternal grandfather. A biblical scholar, Professor of Greek and Hebrew, he was the grandfather I never knew. I was born long after his death. The stories my parents told me about him drew me close to him in admiration and awe. In childhood dreaming I often pondered what could it be like to be in his shoes? A person of impeccable character, a preacher of the Word, a teacher of righteousness. Just looking at his photograph and reading the old copies of the announcements of his lectures on Scripture seemed to pass something of him on to me. I think my admiration of him and his values, as I understood them to be, somehow influenced me with a desire to become like him. The meaning of his life touched my spirit with a yearning for similar purpose and resolve. Dietrich Bonhoeffer has said: "There is meaning in every journey that is unknown to the traveler." Hearing stories of my grandfather influenced my journey to ministry in ways that were clouded in mystery.

I do believe that often children very early in life can exhibit certain characteristics which can be identified as inclinations toward the spiritual and the things of God's kingdom. My desire to know God and to search for God played a major part in my preparation for hearing the divine call. In 1950 when I was nine years old, my parents converted to Catholicism taking me with them. At this time a Roman Catholic Sister, a Dominican, came into my life. She instructed me for my first Holy Communion and Penance, introducing me to a new world. She told me stories about the saints, real people whose lives of courage and faith inspired me. From her descriptions, I was able to imagine new roles of service to God and God's people: St. Francis and the animals, St. Therese and the little way, St. Catherine and the conquest. This Sister taught me how to pray the Catholic prayers of the Hail Mary and the Glory Be. Her teachings and gentle encouragement touched my hungering spirit with awe of the mysteries of grace.

I liked to pray, a discovery made in the transition to the Catholic faith. My imagination was fired by the stories of saints and the mystique of the Mass. Along with me, my brother and parents were also discovering the gifts of Catholic beliefs. I have rich memories of those times when my parents would call us to kneel in prayer, saying the Rosary. I loved the daily Mass which I attended prior to the beginning of classes. I was going to the Catholic School then and the favorite part of my day was this early Mass. I savored the stories of the Church, the rituals of Roman worship, the smells of burning incense and lit candles. I volunteered to assist the Sisters in the cleaning of the sanctuary and frequently rejoiced in the silence of the empty church while I changed altar clothes and polished candlesticks. Even though this seemed to be a natural domain for me, I experienced a mixture of feelings in this conversion to Catholicism. I remembered well the Protestant world of my grandparents, and often I found my mind drifting back to summer nights and childhood depictions of my grandfather.

Reading the Bible made me mindful of my familial predecessors and fascinated me as well. Much of it did seem strange and escaped my understanding. I think I merely liked the feel of the Bible in my hands.

There were early evidences of my desire to serve the Lord. There must be certain gifts, charisms which can be seen. The first of these, I believe, was the desire to read the Word. During my pre-teens, we lived in the country for awhile. Often in those days, I would take my Bible and read to my goats. I liked to imagine I was preaching to a field of people. The story of St. Francis first told to me by the Dominican Sister stayed on my mind. Once I went to the woods close to the pasture where my goats grazed and there I erected a little shrine. I wished to honor this saint. I nailed a cardboard cross to a tree and printed underneath it in crayon letters the words: "St. Francis of Assisi." Here I sat in the cool of the shade, reading scriptures and watching the goats, very much like what I imagined St. Bernadette of the movie, "The Song of Bernadette" to have shepherded. Years later, long after this land had been sold by my parents and I was living as a young wife in another city, I read of a new church having been dedicated in this very spot of my childhood shrine. The name of the new church was St. Francis of Assisi!

All of my life I have been drawn toward helping others to be reconciled with themselves and with one another. I have been especially attracted to the less fortunate. I believe in retrospect that this desire, this charism, was also instrumental in my formation for ministry. Near to the land where we lived there was the home of tenant farmers. Sometimes I walked over there just to be with them. There was something in their poverty which drew me. I ate their raw turnips, chased their pigs, played with the children in the cotton fields and helped them watch for the hidden snakes while we paused and picked blackberries. I didn't give them anything but myself. I gave this companionship simply because I wanted to. I may have needed them far more than they needed me.

Another indication of my desire to help others came in my High School years when I would leave after classes to go to the School for the Blind. I was moved to compassion by the plight of the first graders who were facing their initial separation from home and family. I would line up some of them and we would walk to the park where I shepherded them as I had watched over my goats in earlier days. This desire to care for others was strong in me as a girl. It sprang from a deep well of compassion and the need to respond to others' needs by human caring. Today, my ministry as a hospital chaplain proclaims the same message of being with those in need of compassion.

The hearing of my call to minister came to me in stages. It was a process. The people and events of my childhood were parts of this process. In the grace, unfolding, I have been empowered to look back and see what God was doing in the molding of my person. Like pieces in a puzzle, the memories fall together in a picture of captured grace, one stage blending into another. When I was in high school I thought for awhile about becoming a foreign missionary. This desire stuck with me for several years. During this time I corresponded with the Mother General of Maryknoll. I wrote to her of my dreams to follow Christ, to be as Paul has written, an ambassador of Christ. She wrote back to me, letters of a missionary, inflaming my spirit with the envisioning of total service to God and God's people. That dream faded in time, but the vision remained.

In my ministry this missionary spirit calls forth compassioning for the lonely, the alienated, the marginalized and the rejected.

When I graduated from Catholic High School I entered a new world. I left the tribal village by enrolling in a Southern Baptist College. I had, in this move, come back into the Protestant environs of my youth. Here at Meredith College I heard once again the old hymns of "Amazing Grace" and "Whispering Hope." I took Old and New Testament scripture studies and once more found the treasure of my heart in the Living Word. At first, I had a difficult time reading Scripture critically as I was finding new and different ways of looking at God and creation. It did seem as though some of the old order had passed away for me and I had begun to think more reflectively. I yearned then for reconciliation between churches and was pained by doctrinal differences which kept my Catholic world separated from my Protestant one. I attended the chapel services at college with eagerness as I listened attentively to the President of Meredith and other Baptist preachers who spoke to us. I saw how the scriptures were read in these services as applied teachings to daily life. Memories of these chapel experiences served me well when I began in later years to plan my own chapel services. There was no way for me to know in those days as a college student that I would someday be a minister. There *was* no curriculum for the female pastor. I took the Religion courses available and then moved into the field of Education. I had no concept of pursuing my dream of preaching and shepherding. I decided to be a teacher. In the Catholic Church there was no role for me to aspire to in the line of ministry. I knew that men could be priests, women could be teachers.

I was married in my last semester of college. Although this marriage ended in divorce, this experience and the grace of motherhood formed for me the preparation for my later ministerial role. The skills of the shepherdess were perfected during these years. I learned what it is to minister not by going away to a seminary, but simply by staying and pastoring my children. The word "mother" is defined in Webster's Dictionary as one who "nurtures." The same dictionary defines shepherdess as one who "tends." To be the one is to learn how to become the other and so it was for me. With each birth of the six children, I took another step in the process of my ministerial formation. This is, indeed, a magnificent preparation and I am most grateful for it. I knew my little sheep and they knew me.

Mothering changed me, transforming me in ways of grace I am just now comprehending. In this light I saw how all is done by God. Hearing the first cry of the newborn, celebrating the victory of potty training, getting those first spoonfuls of vegetables down, tying shoelaces, sitting up all night with a sick child, waiting through a son's surgery, sleeping in backyard tents, crying through First Communions, waking in dread to the ringing of the midnight phone, rejoicing at the graduations, crying at the weddings, and always in the process of holding on and letting go.

In these years of child rearing, I was deeply involved in my parish. I had returned to the tribal village where I served as Faith Formation Teacher, Eucharistic Minister, and Homebound Visitor. I had the women's group meeting in my home weekly where we sat around my dinner table and read scripture, invited local clergy to speak and watched our children playing. In my home I often had home Masses where the round dining table became the altar of the Lord. Once a bishop of our diocese offered Mass at this table. I hosted many parish meetings and many of the dishes in my kitchen were those left by covered-dish bearers. "Bryna's House" was frequently the answer to the question, "Where are we meeting?" I cherished my parish community and friends. Many of my closest friends during this time were parish priests and religious women. I believe it was this initial bonding with others of like vision that helped to shape my perception of the co-ministry I do today with pastors and ministers.

For awhile I was actively involved in the Catholic ecumenical and charismatic movement. Prayer meetings were held occasionally in my home. During this experience I was graced with a new openness to the motion of the Holy Spirit. This was essential to the process of my preparation for hearing the call to minister. I saw what God can do in unexpected ways for those who will only believe, and this awareness made me more readily susceptible to the doing of the presumed impossible. In this Spirit, I saw that with God all things are possible if we but love God. This conviction led me a distance from doctrine into the mysterious realm of grace. It was in this light that I learned to trust God as my ultimate authority. It was this authority I was to one day claim as primary in my personal response in becoming a female pastor.

I had left my teaching position in secondary education to be a full-time mother. I did some substitute teaching and often volunteered to teach reading at the Catholic School. I delivered Meals on Wheels and took Communion to the sick. These activities kept alive my vision of serving others for God.

My story took an interesting twist in the middle '80s when I was inadvertently caught up in a controversy involving the washing of the feet. It had come to my attention that the pastors in our diocese had been instructed not to wash the feet of women in the Holy Thursday Liturgy. This information caused me inner pain. I simply could not comprehend how women could be perceived as being those excluded from this sacred invitation to discipleship. From the well of my pain I wrote a poem in which I expressed my feelings. The poem was published by our local diocesan paper and was noticed by the *National Catholic Reporter.* I was asked to be interviewed for this national publication. My picture was taken and was printed on the front page of the *National Catholic Reporter* along with our bishop's. We were presenting two opposing views on this delicate issue of footwashing. I was also contacted during this time by a local group planning a vigil light protest. It was very difficult for me to decide whether or not to march in the protest or to attend the Mass at the Cathedral. I felt torn by my devotion to the Holy Thursday liturgy and my consciousness of justice in the issue of women's exclusion. I ended up doing both that night. I left the vigil light procession around the Cathedral just long enough to attend the Mass inside. Afterwards, as the Bishop left the church, I met him and we exchanged our thoughts about the events of the protest. The result of this encounter between the Bishop and me was the setting up of a series of private dialogue sessions between the two of us. I met with him in his office where we discussed church teachings and women's issues. In the process he and I became friends. He never changed his mind and I kept my same thoughts. The following year, however, priests in our diocese were instructed to decide the issue of allowing participation of women in this ritual for themselves. Over half of the parishes permitted the washing of women's feet. The old order had begun to pass away and I saw that all had been done by God. Imagine! What grace for an ordinary lay woman to dialogue in many sessions with a bishop she had once brought to national attention. Reconciliation took on a new meaning for me, an understanding I was to recognize many times in the work of my chaplaincy.

My childhood dreams of helping the less fortunate never died. As my children grew and were active in school, I found myself volunteering two days a week at the Catholic hospital in our city. Mercy Hospital was run by the Sisters of Mercy, and I enjoyed my work with them. Here I was functioning in the role of "Patient Visitor." I worked as a volunteer with the Pastoral Care Department. I received a list of patients each morning that I volunteered and I visited them in their hospital rooms. I learned listening skills which came naturally to me as I had a keen appreciation for each person's story. I delighted in listening and pointing out where I saw God in their life stories. In this ministry, I came to witness life and death as a wholeness, and I gleaned a respect for the faith of those who were in the process of suffering and loss. One day the Director of Volunteers sent me to a seminar given by the chaplain of another hospital. During his presentation this chaplain mentioned a program of education for hospital chaplains. I knew when I heard the word that I wanted to be a chaplain. The trouble was, I didn't know how. How could I ever do this?

I began by talking with this chaplain after his talk. I asked him if someone like me could be considered for the program, and he told

me to ask for an initial interview with the Director of the Clinical
Pastoral Education program at Carolinas Medical Center. I immediately called and made an appointment. I went with great apprehen-
sion, feeling somewhat presumptuous. I knew that the usual applicant
was ordained or soon to be ordained for ministry. And here I was
a Catholic woman who was not ordained and could never expect to
be so. During the interview I was asked about my experiences in
ministry and I told about my parish and hospital voluntary work.
As she described the clinical educational program in hospital ministry, I knew I had to be there! I felt as though this was where I was
meant to be even though I knew I was in the unique position of
having little possibility of being accepted. I had never been to a
seminary. I don't know what motivated the Director to make the
decision she did, but I do know that the part of my story which
related to the position I took with the bishop over the footwashing
issue interested her. She had read about me in the *National Catholic
Reporter*. I realized that even when we make decisions which pain
us as mine had, when we do what we believe in conscience to be
right, when we move in the Spirit, good things come from it. We
are set free in new truth. One of the fruits of that wrenching time
of protest was my acceptance into the Clinical Pastoral Education
program! What amazing grace it is to have another door opened after
one has closed.

Somewhere along the way in my journey to the hearing of my
personal call to ministry, I had learned to stand for justice. This was
important learning.

I took four units of Clinical Pastoral Education at the Carolinas
Medical Center, completing my ministry there within the residency
program. During this time, I learned pastoring skills of interpersonal
exchange, interdisciplinary teamwork, crisis intervention, counseling, praying, spiritual assessing. I learned how to conduct funeral
services and lead graveside services. I baptized dying babies and took
Holy Communion to Catholics. I discovered my own style of preaching after many attempts to deliver a good homily. I led prayer services
in the chapel and saw my flaws in the videos taken during my services
and discussed them later at the worship seminars. I was assigned to
cancer, neo-natal and heart units. I learned to assess properly the
spiritual and emotional needs of patients and families as well. During
my nights of being "on-call" I quickly acquired skills of pastoring
an entire hospital population inclusive of staff and visitors. The days

rapidly turned to weeks and then to months as I grew into the role
and function of the hospital minister doing the work of the chaplain.

There was much study accompanying this practical ministering.
While in this program I read contemporary theologians such as Karl
Barth and Karl Rahner. I learned in pastoral studies how to develop
my own theological thinking in the appreciation of writers such as
Wayne Oates and Elizabeth Johnson. I studied the Family Systems
of Pastoral Counseling and the psychological theory of Object Relations.

Throughout my two years of study and practice I was under
constant supervision. There were peer seminars to attend in which
we confronted and affirmed one another. We had weekly supervisory
sessions with our supervisors as well. We were required to write
verbatims in which we painstakingly detailed our thoughts, actions,
and visions of our ministering. The units assigned to me became in
a real sense my parish and I became in just as real a sense, the pastor.
I made many referrals to patients' church pastors when they declared
church membership. Frequently, however, my ministry was to those
estranged, alienated or never members of any church or temple. To
these my understanding of justice and reconciliation played a major
role. One of my deepest joys was to see a patient reconciled with
his church or welcomed into one for the first time as a result of my
efforts of reconciliation between church and patient.

During this time I heard God calling me to ministry. It was an
actual event. One night while I was on call, I returned to the chaplains' on-call room after having answered many beeps throughout
the night; sounds from my beeper indicating numbers within the
hospital I was to call. Answering these beeps sent me to the trauma
areas, to the cardiac unit, to the emergency room, to the cancer floor.
Patients and families in distress needed the Chaplain's Word. Returning weary from the patients' needs, I had just taken off my shoes
and lain down on the bed. I knew the morning would not break
until the beeper had sounded again, but for these brief moments
there was silence. I remembered my thoughts as a child when I
pondered: where did the lightning bugs go when the day came? I
had started to drift into sleep when the beeper sounded. Answering
the call, I heard the nurse on the phone saying, "Someone needs you.
Come. Come now." Hearing the words "someone needs you," I
immediately responded. Leaning over to put my shoes back on, my
eyes wandered to the window through which I could see the lights
of the hospital rooms. I thought this must be how the glow of the

lightning bugs continues even in the day. Their light must be given away in their free flight to light. Over there, in that hospital, someone needed ME. The realization struck me powerfully. There was no one to answer that need that night except me. I was the one called! I was the shepherdess hearing the cries of the sheep. I knew in my heart in those moments that I would spend the rest of my life in a ministry lived out in the seeking of the lost sheep, in the returning of that one to the fold of faith. I heard clearly in that night that it was I, Bryna, being called and being sent. The phone rang again. It was the same nurse. "Chaplain Bozart?" she called me by name. "I'm coming" was my response, and I've been responding ever since. The glow of the earliest heart's desire to serve others for God does not go out. It goes forth and loses self in order to gain the whole world.

Before I left this Center I had a crucial conversation with one of my supervisors. I told her that I wanted to be a woman in ministry, but that the chances for future pastoral work were not good for me. Lacking the opportunity for ordination due to my Catholic tradition, I couldn't see how I could continue after completing my residency in chaplaincy. She suggested to me then that I pursue an advanced degree in theological and pastoral studies. I told her I would, but I didn't know how it would be possible. Time passed and I kept her suggestion in my heart.

I graduated from the clinical and pastoral educational program. Several of my children came. They blessed me with their joy. I was also given a special commissioning service by the faculty and it was participated in by my chaplain peers. This was a highlight of grace for me. I was given this ceremony of celebration because it was known that I would not be formally recognized by my church in ordination as the other graduates had or would be. I felt the confirming of my call in this special service as I heard the words of my ministerial peers and experienced the benediction of their affirmation.

Upon closure of this chapter in my life, two significant and powerfully graced events occurred. I was employed as a staff chaplain at the Mercy Hospital in Charlotte, N.C., and I was accepted into the Masters Degree Program at Loyola University in New Orleans. I was the first laywoman ever to be hired as a chaplain at the Catholic hospital where I once volunteered! I was approved for study in the Loyola Institute for Ministry's Extended Program. I could attend classes at a local meeting place while under the direction of Loyola University. In this degree, Masters of Pastoral Studies, I was to study

Old and New Testaments, the concept of ministry, cultural and traditional impacts upon ministry, grace and sacraments, professional pastoral skills and institutional analysis. I learned how to think reflectively in theological discoursing and to write concise, referenced papers. I developed my theology of ministry further in greater detail, relying heavily on Richard McBrien, Thomas F. O'Meara, O.P. and Richard Gula. I studied moral theology and Christian ethics, applying my learning to the practical setting of my chaplaincy.

I believe there have been two factors contributing greatly to my employment at Mercy Hospital. The first was my deep compassion for people in need, a trait of character evidenced by my years of volunteered service. The second was my friendships with others in ministry, the priests and sisters of my diocese, as well as ministers of other denominations.

I began my association with the Sisters of Mercy when I worked in parish ministry with them and continued my friendships with various Sisters as I visited their infirmary and attended retreats and gatherings at their Motherhouse in Belmont, North Carolina. These Sisters have always been encouraging to me. As I began my days of volunteering in the hospital, the Sisters of Mercy welcomed me and companioned me, their trust and belief in me so strong that they offered me the position of chaplaincy. Later, this belief and confidence in me was again seen as I was promoted to the position of Director of Pastoral Care, making me the first laywoman to be in charge of this department.

I have had a long history of friendships with various parish priests as they gave me roles of ministry to perform: Eucharistic Minister, Religious Education Teacher, and Hospice Co-ordinator for the parish. In recent years my friendships with particular Jesuits has led me far into the graced Ignatian spiritual exercises and the consolation of their supportive friendships. My association with those committed to the Church and its mission has enforced my own vision of service. I think these relational aspects played a vital part in my coming to minister within the Catholic setting.

I was known personally by my own people. They liked me and I liked them. My work as a chaplain is a varied and complex ministry. I feel my greatest affirmation as a woman who pastors comes from those to whom I minister. I have never been refused or poorly received. There have been incidences in which my pastoral identity has been questioned. I think this is because traditionally and culturally many people are still perceiving the ministerial role as a male one. Once I was asked to see a patient who wanted to see the chaplain. When I arrived at his room, he looked at me in disbelief. "I want the chaplain," he stated. I told him I was the chaplain. He nodded his head as if to dismiss me, saying, "I want the REAL chaplain." I told him I was the real chaplain. For a few moments there was a silence while he openly stared at me. "You're a woman." he stated. I told him that was true, I was a woman and I was the chaplain. "How can you be?" he asked. I knew the question because it was the one I had asked. Then I told him how it was and how I had come to be who I am. He told me he had never thought about it. We talked about our common faith traditions and I told him how there was a time when I had not thought about it either. We discussed his illness then and conversed for awhile about his situation. I prayed for him. When I started to leave, he took my hand and pointing to his Bible asked me to read something from it. I read him the psalm about not being afraid and we spoke about trusting God in all things. As I was leaving, he said, "Come back tomorrow . . . Chaplain."

Most of the time my ministry is accepted without hesitation. It just doesn't seem to matter that I am a woman. Suffering and fear experienced by patients seems to erase nonsensical barriers and cuts to the core of things. Christ's love is genderless.

Once in a Sunday morning Worship Service I was leading, a woman read from her wheelchair. Her biblical selection was from Romans 8:28, "And we know that all things work together for good to them that love God, to them who are called according to God's purpose." This gives the meaning of my life's calling. I love to conduct these interfaith worship services which are held in the hospital's rehabilitation center. This is open to the patients, families, and staff of the hospital. I am always blessed when I minister here. We sing hymns, tell our faith stories, read from Scriptures, pray for ourselves and others, and give God glory and praise. We come just as we are: patients sometimes in wheelchairs, I.V. tubes trailing, families in bunches of worry and grace, staff taking a break from the floors, physicians coming and going, and myself standing before them, proud to be one of them, much humbled to be the shepherdess of such a magnificent flock. I keep my sermons brief and to the point so as to allow times for reflections to be shared from the congregation. We may also be blessed with an unplanned altar call when someone wants to come forward and ask for Jesus to come more fully into her life. Sometimes we may experience a movement of the Spirit when several persons will band together and lay hands upon a patient to pray for him. Our worship is as varied as the participants, coming from diverse cultures, traditions, races, creeds and socioeconomic levels. We come together for one purpose: to share our faith and love for God, to worship God in communion and to ask God's tender mercy in our lives. These services and these people never cease to bless me and my calling with abundant grace.

There have been difficult times, deep waters to cross, in the journey. I don't think the people back in the pews of my Catholic parishes always understand me or know what it is that I do. I realize that there must be more education within the Church regarding the role and functions of women called by God to minister. Catholics, like other male-oriented denominations, have traditionally looked upon specific ministerial positions to be exercised solely by men. There have been times when a Catholic will come to my office, read the sign "Chaplain" over the door, and assume I am the secretary. "Where is the chaplain?" will be the query. I am accustomed to this. I understand the conditioning behind it. Gently, very gently, I attempt to lead them through the puzzlement, the gray areas, to meet this new day. I do wish that more could be spoken from the pulpit generally about what is going on in the arena of ministry today. Many Catholics don't know that Roman Catholic theology and ministry are increasingly lay, not clerical, endeavors. Many women have in recent years received graduate degrees in theology, usually a Masters of Divinity. Already we see women within the present church structure functioning in roles of Religious Education Directors and Pastoral Associates. The average Catholic needs to know that these women have been highly educated and formed for ministry. They, too, have heard a call by God to which they have responded. It does pain me that these women lack public recognition and celebration. There is a deep water of confusion of identity and a drowning sense of frustration we are going through. This is due to the vagueness of our pastoral authority which needs to be defined openly by those in teaching positions within the Church.

I have been asked many times to speak to Protestant Sunday School classes, senior citizens, and congregations about life as a chaplain, but rarely do such invitations come from home. I feel in this respect, a stranger among my own. I try to remember in these situations that my ultimate authority is God and that all works for good in God's time. I am reminded of the hymn "How Firm a Foundation": "When through the deep waters I call thee to go, the rivers of sorrow shall not overflow."

I need to make it clear, however, that I am acknowledged and approved by the Catholic Church for ministry. I have received formal credentials for chaplaincy. I have a letter of endorsement from our bishop, recommending me for ministry. In the amazing grace of my story's theme, I am honored to have a personal letter of endorsement written by the bishop who became a friend in the deep waters of the footwashing controversy. God does work for good because we love God. This endorsement is a requirement of The National Association of Catholic Chaplains who have given me certification. To obtain this certification, I had to present a written summary of how I believed I had met the standards and competencies of this association. I had to gather verbatims written in my years of study and practice, along with letters of recommendation from supervisors and department heads. Taking all these papers I had to appear before a evaluating committee and orally answer their questions and concerns. It is not an easy process and certification cannot be readily assumed. Receiving my paper of certification by The National Association of Catholic Chaplains was a highlight in my pastoral and professional journey. This certification is reviewed by the Association every five years.

Today I am the Director of the Pastoral Care Department at Mercy Hospital. I am assisted in this ministry by the Sisters of Mercy. A day does not pass that my heart is not touched by grace. It is good to be here. This is a busy, ever changing mission. Every day is different. My office door is always open and I never know who or what concerns will cross my threshold. I meet often with the hospital Ethics Committee as well as the regional Resource Board of Bioethics. I continue to seriously study moral theology and Christian ethics. I invite various local speakers into our hospital setting to speak to our staff on matters of spirituality and emotional well-being. I work hard to co-ordinate local clergy participation in our hospital ministry and have come to call many my friends. I am a member of the city's Clergy Association and am involved in the County's Ministerial Association. I am called upon by these organizations to speak to the community as well as to local churches on matters of ethical decisions and spirituality in the modern world. I have a particular interest in the plight of persons with AIDS. and I serve as a facilitator for the regional AIDS. interfaith network organization. These activities focus me outward beyond the confines of my ministry setting into the world of communal compassion. This outreach, I do believe, is essential to the balancing of a minister's vision and mission. Like the Church, we are also called to go forth into the world, to give benediction there and to be blessed ourselves.

It is in the world of the faith communities that I am brought most forcefully up against the deep waters of misunderstanding caused by my lacking ordination. Obstacles surface in my course. It is interesting to me to note that when we come together as Christians to worship, as seen in my Sunday Interfaith Service, reconciliation and ecumenism just happen. I see this as God's action. We are participating in a ministry of the Spirit which is the living out of the prayer Jesus prayed when he asked that we all be one. When I responded to the call to minister to the lost sheep, to go out to all in need regardless, I began to move and act in this vision of Christ, a vision for ministry. "All has been done by God who has reconciled us to God through Christ and has given us the ministry of reconciliation. I mean that God, in Christ, was reconciling the world to God, not counting people's transgressions against them, and that God has entrusted the message of reconciliation to us. This makes us ambassadors for Christ, God as it were appealing through us." (2 Cor. 5:17-20) All of my ministry, all that I am as one so called, is totally devoted to this commission.

I believe any barriers I experience come in forms relating to the lacking of ordination. I should be clear on one point. I am not presently, nor have I ever sought ordination in the existing Catholic structure. I do, however, by virtue of my calling, engage in priestly ministry. I see my Catholic baptism as a means of being enjoined in what Vatican II has named "the royal priesthood of the faithful." I see that the ministry that I do is readily affirmed by the people to whom I minister. In ecumenical participation, I sometimes encounter problems. I am, at times, embarrassed by the lacking of ordination which causes considerable confusion. When I am asked to participate in a Lutheran or Methodist service, for example, or when I am asked to preach in a non-Catholic church, the question of "robing" invariably comes up. All the ministers don robes except me. I have not been able to robe because I have not had a robe. This lacking, which may seem like a small thing, does cause consternation on the part of the other ministers. What should be done about me? Will I stand out as vastly different from the others? Should I? Usually a robe is located in the sacristy for me. In this situation I am touched by the compassion of my fellow/sister ministers and their actions of grace.

It is confusing because when one denomination fully empowers women in ministry and another does not, and the woman is engaging

in ecumenical roles of ministry in varying faith settings, she is forced
to modify her functions according to the tradition she is ministering
with. There are no universal expectations for her. I find myself
constantly evaluating my public role and function. My male colleagues are not so challenged. When I, to give an example, am invited
to preach in a church as the guest preacher, I have to be mindful of
such things as location. Where can I stand while I am talking to the
congregation? Can I stand behind the pulpit or is this location
off-limits in this church? Sometimes even the title of my reason for
being there has to be carefully worded. Can I call my sermon a
sermon? Does it have to be named as a "reflection." Can I preach in
this faith tradition as a woman or does my preaching have to be
called something else because women traditionally cannot preach in
this particular church?

As an interfaith minister within the hospital setting, much of
my ministry is to people of all faiths. Sometimes I am asked to anoint
people with oils. This is seen in their faith as an aid to their healing.
I have "anointed" Pentecostals, for example, and yet I cannot anoint
a dying Catholic, even when a priest cannot be located in time. There
have been times when I have conducted funerals as previously mentioned, but I cannot con-celebrate a Catholic Mass at the funeral
service. I am just as privileged to read a scripture at a Catholic funeral
as I am to lead a Protestant one. I note these varying roles simply
to illustrate the degree of confusion which exists in the ecumenical
arena where one ordains women and the other does not.

I don't see unity among Christians coming from dialogues and
discussions about doctrinal differences as clearly as I see unity spring-
ing from shared charisms. I don't think the issue is as much about
differences relating to ordination as it is about our response in loving
God. However, what I think is not so important. What is important
is the working of God towards good in the lives and hearts of all
those who first love God. This action is one of the Holy Spirit which
can be seen today in our worship. It springs from the ordinary. It
bubbles forth from the fountain of the sort of grace lived by good
people. I was privileged to see this kind of action while on a recent
pilgrimage to the Holy Land. I had gone with a group of Lutheran
and Catholic folks. I witnessed there a transcending grace when in
a special hour of worship on sacred ground, these two denominations
were led by their respective priests into an historical event of Christian unity. In this Liturgy of the Eucharist I saw us become one –
one in Spirit – as the Spirit of the Risen Jesus came to meet us while

we were coming to meet him. This is how it happens. What role I play, what functions I perform or what others may do is not so important. We take ourselves far too seriously. What is to be taken seriously is the sacred in the ordinary. What matters is what God calls us to be and to do. Sometimes, in grace, we are and we do. An old, dying patient once said to me, "Look up, Baby. Keep your eyes on the Lord. Look up. The rest is no matter at all."

In the Catholic structure, ordination is a means of obtaining and keeping power. The ordained lead in ritual, dispense sacraments and grace, make the important decisions. I think we need to take a look at power as held in our system. Ministry is about servanthood. The shepherdess brings her flock together as one, when she serves their needs and not her own. My ministry sheds new light on old truths. We are gifted by God to minister. Each time I hear the "confession" of a patient, for example, I am mindful of the privileged role I play as an instrument of God's peace.

Forgiveness doesn't need absolution. While it would be helpful to have the stole of the priest, it is not a necessity for me. As I have learned to pass easily among the barriers of my church's centralized structure, strong ecclesiology and sacramental emphasis, I have also learned to be at peace with undeveloped ecclesiology working with churches stressing conversion and sanctification. I don't dialogue ecumenism. I live ecumenism in the service that I render.

I am on the journey of the shepherdess, a journey taking me deep into the ecumenical experience. It is an experience of grace and not anything less than this. It avoids discussion of doctrinal differences when they become barriers of mere debate. It encourages cherishing one's tradition while deeply respecting another's. A shepherdess knows she is the stewardess and not the owner of her flock. She trusts her sheep's relationship with their God. She plays out her role in nurturing that relationship in the many avenues it may take.

The shepherdess never shepherds alone. Her voice calls out to others in ministry. They come to help her in her need. On the occasions when, as a resident chaplain, I had to perform weddings for staff and patients, I had to seek the assistance of my ordained colleagues. This was because a non-ordained minister cannot marry persons in our State. I have been deeply touched to witness the caring companionship extended to me in this situation by my fellow/sister ministers. Some one of them would stand quietly by my side as I performed the wedding ceremony, only to step forward at the end to sign the legal papers. I believe this sort of co-ministry, this deep level of ministerial companionship on the mutual journey, is the core of ecumenism.

There are humorous moments. Once a Navy Recruiter came to my office and stopped in mid-sentence. "I wanted to talk to you about . . . you're a woman!" He had not anticipated a female pastor. End of discussion. Chaplains in the military have to be ordained. The Catholic Church won't do this for me. Nothing more to say. I don't see the question as being one that asks if I want to be in the military. I see the question as being one that ponders: do I have the freedom to serve all peoples for the love of God?

I do have faith that God is working all things for good. There are places of holy ground, people of holiness among us. Look and see. There is a Holy Land within our hearts. There are those who search for justice. Blessed are they. Pastors who go out of their way to be ecumenical, to give women within their churches ministerial roles. Once in a while we hear of a Catholic bishop who has assigned the position of Pastoral Associate to a woman. We see in Catholic parishes altar girls where once only boys served. Women have come as close to the door closed to ordination as possible. We remain at the door which does seem to me to be decaying on a crumbling frame. Something has to give. It will.

It seems to me that women called to ministry in this new day are examples of persons of radical grace, a grace that irritates in the sense that we by our lives of service, excite and stimulate growth in new theological thought. We minister in a tension that is of the movement of the Holy Spirit. My story is a story of the experience of this irritating, but gentle grace.

Recently a Professor Emeritus of Religious Studies lovingly gave me his academic robe to wear in services. This gift reminded me of another. When my mother died, a Jesuit friend took off his priestly stole and gave it to me to wear at her graveside service. I am blessed, a hundredfold.

The voice of the shepherdess may be heard in parish and hospital corridors, in ecumenical services and whispered in prayer. The voices I most remember hearing, however, are those of my children calling out to me from the crowd in the auditorium of Loyola University as I received my pastoral studies degree. "We love you, Mom. You did it, Mom. Way to go!" It is a good way to go. It is the way of grace.

It is the winding, unexplored and challenging path of the gentle shepherdess.

2

The Journey of a Modern Pioneer

Rev. Liz Dikkers Killeen

How do you tell the story of your life – of how you were born, how you lived, and how you knew which choices to make to fulfill your destiny? "A long time ago," you might say, because there is something magic about "long ago" beginnings, especially as the years go by and you grow older and reflect on the past. But it is not my "life's" story that I am here to tell. It *is* my life's story as it relates to my relationship with God and my call to professional church leadership. This relationship with my God, so awesome, so mysterious, so real is an active one, as I continue to be profoundly affected by the Lord's presence in my life and my call to pastoral ministry.

Born in Stillwater, Minnesota to the family of a Baptist minister, I learned at a young age the commitment of my parents to servant leadership. This commitment strongly influenced my own spiritual growth as I experienced the practical side of pastoral ministry.

I remember as a very young child waiting for my father to pick me up from school so I could accompany him on his afternoon round of calls. Both my parents demonstrated the love of God and at an early age I came to a saving knowledge of a loving and compassionate God. I accepted the role of "preacher's kid" with pride. Others of my siblings did not!

During both Junior and Senior High School I was actively involved in the church and youth work. I served as an officer for both local and state youth groups.

Going to college was not a choice in our family – it was expected. It was also expected that if you were a girl your fields were limited to teaching or nursing. I chose teaching and majored in Speech and Drama with a minor in French and English. I taught Speech and French for one year in a small town in Iowa in the '60s. It was not the place for a 21 year old single women to be teaching Plato! After one year I left for the East Coast to begin graduate studies while teaching "special education" in the public school.

It was there that I met and married the man with whom I would spend the next eleven years. Our daughter was born the following year. As a Christian the word divorce was not a part of my vocabulary. When it became a reality, my world was crushed and it took years of healing to mend the brokenness of my life. That healing did not take place until after I spent time abusing my freedom.

But I sought the Lord and the Lord found me and picked me up and called me by name saying, "Sister Liz, I have work for you to do. I have a kingdom that needs to be built on this earth and I'm setting you aside to help me." It was as if I were being immersed in the waters of baptism a second time. I knew my life would never be the same again and that my spiritual journey had really begun. It was both magic and mystical. Scripture promises that a time is coming when God will turn God's face to such as the poor, the captive, the blind, and the oppressed – when the light of God's face will shine on the dark corners where they live. God had turned God's face toward me again and had shined on my dark corners. I began to understand words like "grace" and "forgiveness" and "unconditional love."

This journey was, in retrospect, a preparation for my call to pastoral ministry. My spirit was strengthened throughout these years as I felt God's loving grace work within me.

The benchmark experience involving my actual call to ministry came in the spring of 1982. I had been employed by a large Baptist Church in Massachusetts for nearly fourteen years as office administrator. When parishioners would come in for pastoral counseling I would start a conversation and we would talk while they waited for the pastor. I soon forgot about the work I should have been doing and became people-centered versus task-centered.

One day it came as a sign painted in front of me: "You are on the wrong side of the desk!" The flight to "the Hill" had begun. Andover Newton Theological School is known as the school on the hill. My response was immediate for I had given the call to God who began opening doors of opportunity.

My original concerns were, how do I pay for a seminary education, support my teenage daughter, and run a house while doing the kind of work seminary would require? The first open door was being hired by the Public Relations Department of Andover Newton Theological School as assistant to the director. Tuition was free to employees of the school! My bills would be paid! I still had a regular salary. The biggest sacrifice would be my fourteen-year-old daughter who would be left alone more than a fourteen-year-old should be. She had a boyfriend and soon his family became central to her existence. Our relationship suffered and we have shed many tears over those lost years. I thank God that today she is married to a wonderful man with two beautiful boys and that our relationship has been rebuilt and that we are best friends. Further evidence of God's grace

Must the need to respond to God's call have to come with sacrifices? Perhaps, perhaps not. But God didn't always make it easy for the people of faith who heard God's call and who responded. Nor did God make it easy for me. But I knew I must be obedient and it never occurred to me that I could not respond because I had the wrong anatomy!

Because I felt my "call" to full time Christian service was so real and so divine I may have been wearing blinders as I met with seminary personnel to arrange for enrollment procedures. Blinders not to these people who were so helpful and encouraging, but to certain members of my local church who tried to erect barriers at various stages of my training. I cannot be certain, but suspect that some of the reactions were out of a longing within them to also be training for ministry, but due to their life situations or lack of a college education were not able to respond to their call.

I felt confident of my choice to finish my seminary studies and all obstacles placed before me were soon obliterated.

Those responsible for my training and formation as a minister represented two sources, the seminary staff, especially the professors, and the church family I served after completing one year of "field education." In many ways the seminary professors affirmed women in ministry, treating us as equals in class participation, and with respect. The response of the church was one of total acceptance and affirmation. I was fortunate to serve this church for three years during my training as Student Associate. (The pastor was bivocational). My responsibilities included all of the pastoral calling, hospital visitations and funerals as well as preaching once a month. These experiences drew us close as we shared stories that connected us as a community of faith.

In many ways the seminary environment sheltered women from the realities of the real world and the struggle it would be to find placement upon completion of the Master of Divinity degree. We would be required to work twice as hard as men and we would be evaluated by success or failure in ministry. Women in seminaries do not realize that finding a placement is much harder the second time they seek a change in ministry setting.

I have seen lives transformed by the grace of God as God has called me by name and allowed me to be God's instrument of love and reconciliation to broken lives. It is difficult to realize that not everyone accepts my call to ministry as legitimately from God! If someone visits the church and leaves upon discovering the pastor is a woman they would not benefit from my ministry! This has happened. People have left during worship when they saw me come in robed, my name on the front of the Sunday bulletin. It is usually a young couple carrying an encased bible.

One couple's story is worth telling (I hope). This family had attended worship for a year or so and had joined early in 1995. They had been assimilated into the life of the church in beautiful ways, attending small groups, camping trips, support groups, fellowship and social events. Throughout all of this they affirmed my role as their pastor. That affirmation was shattered by an "issue" that presented itself to the church: the attendance of a lesbian couple. The family left the church and attempted to take others with them without success. Eventually the issue of a woman minister came into play after they talked to a former male pastor, of another denomination, who told them to stay away from any church pastored by a woman.

On the flip side of this has been the tremendous affirmation of both ministries I have been privileged to serve. I was called from seminary *to start* a new church in New Jersey. Our denomination had placed an emphasis on planting new churches and I had been qualified to be a church planter!

Shortly after arriving at this burgeoning new community just outside Princeton the local newspaper editor asked if I would develop a religion section. As a result I was able to write a regular column in the *Plainsboro View*. I addressed such topics as "When We Hurt,"

"God Is Our Closest Friend," "A Creative Approach To Change," "The Pain Within," etc.

From the responses to these articles, support groups were formed, such as a weekly pot-luck dinner for divorced persons, special interest bible studies, and therapy groups for adults seeking to heal emotional wounds from childhood. The singles group mailing list eventually numbered more than 400.

I believe that when we don't have a "stained-glass mentality," we can concentrate on reaching into the brokenness of peoples lives and begin the road to healing.

My second placement was at Grace Baptist of Downers Grove, Illinois. Early in 1990 I was contacted by the Search Committee of Grace Baptist Church of Downers Grove via letter. Not wanting to face the possibility of uprooting and moving to the Midwest (I love the East Coast) I set the letter aside and forgot about it . . . until a month or so later when it was discovered during a routine desk clean-up. I reread the letter and the little booklet that had been prepared for potential pastoral candidates. As I was about to put the book down the word *shepherd* literally jumped from the last page into my psyche. I had just finished a series of sermons on the Psalm 23, and was no doubt oversensitized by the idea that here was a church looking for a pastor-type to be shepherd to them. So intrigued was I, that the process of communication between us began. I responded with a very short letter saying how much the idea of "wanting a shepherd-type pastor" spoke to me. Five months later I flew to Illinois from New Jersey to spend a weekend with the fine folk of Grace Baptist. Someone had worked out a schedule that would allow for a good intake of information about both the people and the place.

Well into my second year of ministry at Grace I realized that I didn't have a clue as to how to mobilize this congregation of "too many chiefs and no Indians" (a self given definition of who they were).

In the summer of 1991 I entered the Doctor of Ministry program at Northern Baptist Theological Seminary in Lombard, Illinois putting my focus on church renewal.

In the fall of 1992, I undertook a project for the Theological Foundations for Ministry Class, which had as its intent to begin the process of equipping laity for ministry: motivating ministry through church renewal. The course required that the pastor and a Congregational Support Committee "engage in theological study, reflection, and engagement in ministry." Together they would endeavor to lead the church to greater understanding of a theology of church renewal and would involve the congregation in developing a plan for renewal of Grace Baptist Church.

After studying the scriptures, the committee and I began to plan ways to involve the entire congregation in understanding the theology of renewal and to provide a policy around which it could focus their efforts to grow and serve. The following vision statement was adopted: The people of Grace Baptist Church of Downers Grove pursue a vision of themselves as a church of caring people led by God bringing others to an experience of love and hope through Jesus Christ.

How were we to lead the congregation in studying the theology of renewal? Using the idea of "caring people bringing others to love and hope," the committee planned a series of Lenten studies with the theme of "Reaching Up and Reaching Out." There were six weeks of study: Reaching Up in Faith, Reaching Up in Hope; Reaching Out with Joy; Reaching Out in Hope; Reaching Out with Care, and Reaching Out with Love. A curriculum was developed. Members of the committee made arrangements for hosts and leaders for five small groups to meet four evenings and one morning during each week. Members of the congregation were invited and assigned to groups.

Following the completion of the Lenten series, the Board of Deacons spent time in analyzing their strengths, weaknesses and opportunities. By looking at how the items identified as "opportunities" related to the vision statement, the committee began to identify areas needing growth: congregation, finance, areas of ministries, and spirituality. In 1993, the congregation adopted long-range goals in each of the categories and recommended that the various church committees develop a working plan for 1994.

One of the long-range goals for 1994 was a 10% increase in worship attendance and church membership. A chart was made showing that each month of 1994 saw an increase in worship attendance over the same month in 1993 except April which stayed the same. The average weekly attendance for the year was 62.2 compared to 53.3 in 1993 for an overall increase of 17%. We had a total of 277 visitors. We gained nine new members. The visitor total of 277 may be misleading for many family members visit from out of town and many are simply church shopping. We have no way of knowing how many do not return because the pastor is a woman. We do know when someone *comes* because the pastor is a woman.

The above statistics led to a brainstorming session with members from the worship and spiritual life committee and at large members who had agreed to develop the 1995 Lenten study series.

As a result of this initial session a theme was adapted: "Are We Ready For Company?" The goal stated: "Through Bible study and exploration together to adopt specific practices for becoming a more inviting people."

Prior to the first session we felt it would be a valuable tool to survey all those who were new to the church within the last four to five years. The following questions were addressed: (1) Who or what invited you to Grace Baptist Church? (2) Once you came, what influenced you to come back again? (3) What special groups within the congregation did you become involved with? (4) If you joined a group, how did the group help you begin to feel a part of the church? (5) What other things happened to help you feel you belonged to the church family? (6) Were there some things you can think of that would have been helpful to you that were not experienced? (7) As a relative newcomer to the congregation, what suggestions can you make for helping us to become more inviting?

The survey was sent to over 30 families – with a nearly 50% returns, 40% of those indicated that the pastor's class was influential in their assimilation into the life of the church.

This was a wake up call for me. I knew I felt passionately about this class as a special element of my ministry. I had no idea those who had gone through the class felt as passionately as I did about it! Here are some of the respondents' comments:

"The class had the balance between being welcoming without being gushing."

"Everyone in the group was supportive, very open, always listening when others spoke, very interesting topics."

"Pastor's class helped with my spiritual journey as an American Baptist."

"I got to know people on a more personal basis; this helped me to feel more a part of the church."

"It helped build relationships where love and concern are shared."

"The spirit was working through Pastor Liz."

"I was convinced that I should be baptized."

"I was able to come in closer contact, on a more personal level with others in the class. She is my pastor and I respect her theology and her guidance."

The pastor's class continues to be a vital tool for helping people feel they belong within the church family and will be the focus for my final project required to complete the Doctor of Ministry Degree.

Women continue to be challenged by what the future holds for us as religious leaders.

"Who knows what women can be when they are finally free to become themselves?"

When Betty Friedan asked this question in *The Feminine Mystique*, scarcely half of the population seemed to care about an answer. But this question raised in 1963 would not go away and the women's movement began.

Like most movements, the struggle spilled over into the church. Although women have been ordained in the USA since 1853, (Antoinette Brown, UCC) it appears that modernity has brought the issue of ordaining women to the front page of the ecclesiastical institution.

The current situation within the American Baptist Churches indicates that there have been many changes in local churches with regard to women in ministry, but progress is slow and uneven. Although the number of women serving as pastors has doubled in the past ten to twelve years, women still face great difficulty finding positions as pastors in settings previously assigned exclusively to men.

The number of women in seminaries has increased dramatically. More women than ever are preparing for pastoral ministry. The majority of our seminaries now report an almost 50-50 ratio of male/female seminarians. More women are being ordained. More Roman Catholic women attend seminaries than ever before.

The church in the future will have to utilize the leadership of women to the fullest, because women are representing an increasingly large proportion of the trained and competent leadership available to the church. Women have a new image of themselves and they will insist that their leadership be recognized.[1]

I would like to attempt to clarify how I see the exclusion of women in ministry to be a carry over tradition from the early Catholic Church where patriarchy was the order of the day. It has since become a conceptual trap for the Roman Catholic Church as well as other denominations.

Many still believe that scripture prohibits the ordination of women. Most often quoted is 1 Timothy 2:11-12: "Let the woman learn in silence with all subjection. But I suffer not a woman to teach, nor to usurp authority over the man, but to be in silence." Another often quoted verse is from 1 Corinthians 14:35: "And if they will learn anything, let them ask their husbands at home: for it is a shame for women to speak in the church."

I would like to address these texts in the hope that a better understanding of them will help remove the obstacles that prevent understanding and reconciliation among the Christian churches.

The first verse clearly seems to say that women ought not have a voice at church meetings say less be ordained as ministers. Church leaders, however, ignore this when hiring church school teachers, youth directors, or Christian Education staff. Without women, both paid staff and laity, the programs of the church would be nonexistent. How does one define the line that separates a woman from teaching and preaching?

One must understand what was going on in the church during the first Christian century. Careful interpretation is important. It seems the women were getting a sense of their freedom in Christ and consequently were asking to stand before God as equals to men. Could this have been an opportunity for them to speak out in church meetings and tell how their husbands were treating them, giving them lectures on how to behave, publicly humiliating them! In the Greco-Roman society this would have been scandalous!

Paul, in his first letter to the Corinthians, was trying to stop this behavior by saying that domestic problems should be dealt with behind the privacy of one's own home and that it was wrong for women to abuse the privileges they had found through Christ's liberation. Paul wanted the early Christians to know that the church was for the purpose of worship and praise to God, not a therapist's couch.

I do not believe that Paul intended for women to be forever excluded from exercising leadership in the church. Just as with men who are behaving scandalously outside the church, so should women doing likewise be forbidden to exercise leadership.

In Luke 23:44-46 we read that the "veil was rent" or the wall that separated the High Priests in the Holy of Holies (which contained the Ark of the Covenant) from the Jewish men in the Holy

Place (reserved for those in Hebraic tradition to be upstanding citizens of God's Kingdom) from the outer court where the Gentiles could worship had fallen down.

The above text says that there was an earthquake when Christ died. That earthquake ripped down the wall the separated the temple dwellers. I believe Paul saw this as evidence that the hierarchical system of the Old Testament had been abolished (see Ephesians 2:14-16). In Christ we are all one "children of God through faith" (Galatians 3:26, *NRSV*). "As many of you who were baptized into Christ have clothed yourselves with Christ. There is no longer Jew or Greek, there is no longer male or female; for all of you are one in Christ Jesus. And if you belong to Christ, then you are Abraham's offspring, heirs according to the promise" (Galatians 3:27-29).

Christ made it possible for all to be equal: Jews, Gentiles and Women. Why has it taken so long for governments and specific cultural societies to follow Christ's example? A burning question for anyone liberated by the work of the Holy Spirit, who is not limited by secular differentiations, but rather imparts gifts to men and women alike.

We read in Acts 2:17-18, "In the last days, it will be, God declares, that I will pour out my Spirit upon all flesh, and your sons and your daughters shall prophesy, and your young men shall see visions, and your old men shall dream dreams. Even upon my slaves, both men and women, in those days I will pour out my spirit; and they shall prophesy."

I do not believe that Peter is suggesting that only men would be the recipients of these gifts, rather it is very clear that women, too, would receive them and whoever receives them is obligated to use them in Christian service.

This New Testament passage has blessed my life and has encouraged me to deepen my life in Christ, through whom a new day has dawned, lifting women and Gentiles to positions once held only by Jewish men.

In his book, *20 Hot Potatoes Christians Are Afraid to Touch,* Tony Campola says, "Recently I spent some time with a Roman Catholic bishop who explained to me how women had been a godsend to many of the churches in his diocese which lacked priestly leadership. He explained that nuns were serving as the pastors for many of his rural congregations, although the people did not actually call them pastors. These nuns visited the sick, taught the catechism, preached the homilies, and even served Holy Communion. He explained that once a month, he or one of his auxiliary bishops would visit each of these female-led parishes, perform the mass, and sanctify the bread and wine. These "sanctified elements" would then be stored until worship time, when they would be given to communicants by the nuns. When I pointed out that these nuns do everything that priests do and therefore should be ordained, he agreed. Then he added, 'Most people in these parishes would also agree, but you know how the church is.' Indeed I do!"[2]

NOTES

1. Elizabeth J. Miller, *Claiming Our Gifts: A Professional Journal For American Baptist Women in Ministry*, Winter 1993, p 27.
2. Anthony Campola, *20 Hot Potatoes Christians Are Afraid To Touch*, Dallas, Word Publishing, 1988, p. 41.

3

The Decision to Ordain

Rev. Meg H. Madson

One Sunday when I was about thirteen, I sat in church listening to what seemed to me an especially boring sermon. "Why, I could do better than this," I thought. The moment passed. I lived through that sermon and adolescence too. Five years later I attended a Lutheran college where I met excellent professors in the religion department, whose lectures about scripture and church history fascinated me. Although I was a dance major, my first love was theology. I happily took electives in the religion department to satisfy my own curiosity, but remained a dance major. After all, I could teach dance, but what could I do with theology? I never imagined that within ten years I would be an ordained Lutheran pastor.

In 1970, while I was absorbed in college life, two American Lutheran churches voted to ordain women.[1] However momentous this decision was in terms of American church history,[2] it caused no earthquake in these Lutheran pews. In fact, at the national convention of the Lutheran Church in America the motion to change the word "man" (that defined the ordered ministry) to "person" passed by a voice vote after only one half-hour of debate![3]

Such a brief period of deliberation might give the impression that the decision to ordain women was made lightly, merely to be in tune with the times. To the contrary, prior to the national conventions in 1970 theological commissions studied at length the scriptural and theological objections to ordaining women. They agreed that the question could not be solved by absolutizing first century attitudes toward women. For example, it would be a misuse of Scripture to claim that women today ought to be veiled in church or forbidden to cut their hair, as were the conditions for first-century women. These Lutheran scholars also agreed that the question of ordaining women could not be decided by considering any special gifts that women *qua* women bring to the ministry, such as enabling and community building, any more than it would be a question of the peculiar skills that men *qua* men might bring to ministry.[4] Women are individuals and differ accordingly. Of course, the distinctive talents and personality that any man or woman has make a difference in the practical performance of ministry, but this is not the reason for ordaining women. Nor should women be ordained simply on the basis of a simplistic argument for equal rights – that just as women can be CEOs or fork-lift drivers, so they should be able to be ordained. Ordination is not a right but a privilege. The only valid reason for ordaining women would have to be the same theological rationale as for ordaining men.

LUTHER ON WOMEN

Martin Luther, of course, never dreamed of ordaining women. But when he encouraged priests to marry and later married himself, he opened the door to a new partnership between men and women based on mutuality and friendship. For centuries Christians valued a life of monastic celibacy more highly than marriage and family. The Reformation challenged this credo. As if to expose an ancient slander, the Reformers left touching portraits of their wives as indispensable companions in ministry. Luther boasted simply: "I would not give up my Katie for France or Venice."[5] The Reformers transferred the accolades previously reserved for celibacy and the monastery to marriage and family life. Karlstadt spoke for many Reformers when he said, "It is better to make a home and teach the Word of God to one's family than to mutter frigid prayers alone in a sanctuary."[6]

Luther, to be sure, was a man of his time and to a large extent viewed women in terms of the needs of his time. In the sixteenth century women were needed to bear and raise many children in order that a few might survive to maturity. The natural restrictions of childbearing meant that women were dependent on and subordinate to men. Luther believed that this natural subordination of women was confirmed by Scripture, as Paul notes in 1 Corinthians 14:34-35.[7] Luther also believed that women did not possess the natural qualities needed for ministry, such as a strong voice, clear expression, and good memory.[8] While these qualities can be developed, such training was simply an unrealistic expectation for the majority of women in the sixteenth century.

Nevertheless, that women needed to devote themselves to children and home did not mean that women could never preach publicly and administer the sacraments. When Luther attacked the clericalism of his day, he asserted that even women serve in the public ministry of the church when they baptize in emergency situations:

> Not only baptism but also preaching and granting absolution can be done by women if men are not available, as is the case in nunneries.[10] Could women administer communion? This sacrament is, to be sure, never an emergency sacrament as baptism can be. And communion is not a more important sacrament than baptism and absolution, since all three sacraments are founded on the same Word of God.[11] Luther even said that there is but one sacrament, Christ, and three sacramental signs (baptism, communion, absolution).[12] Clearly what matters most for Luther is that God's visible and audible Word (Augustine) be proclaimed. The proclaimer/administrator plays a secondary role in the drama of salvation.

CAN WOMEN REPRESENT CHRIST?

Some traditions say "no." The Lutheran Church-Missouri Synod argues on the basis of a biblical literalism that women should not exercise authority over men in the church.[13] The Roman Catholic Church has said "no"[14] because women lack physical similarity to Jesus. Only males can assume the iconic role of representing Christ in the Eucharist. If ordained ministry means re-presenting Christ, the logic of the Catholic position is compelling. Some feminists agree with Catholic doctrine that ministry means re-presentation. In order to include women as representatives of Christ, they emphasize that clergy represent Jesus' humanity and that his sex and race are secondary matters. The problem with this position is that by de-emphasizing the particularity of Jesus as a first century male Jew, this view tends toward Gnosticism.[15]

LUTHER ON MINISTRY

What has been decisive for twentieth century Lutherans facing the question of ordaining women is Luther's view of priesthood and public ministry. In place of the distinction between priest and layman, Luther affirmed the priesthood of all believers. No special spiritual callings or special gifts of grace set Christians apart from one another: "All baptized women are the spiritual sisters of all baptized men, having the same sacrament, spirit, faith, spiritual gifts and goods. . . ."[16] All baptized Christians are given the command, "Go make disciples of all nations. . . ." All are authorized to proclaim the promises of Christ whatever their station in life.

Yet within the church some Christians are called to the *public* ministry of Word and sacrament. The Gospel itself gives definition and identity to the public office.[17] The whole notion is as simple and pragmatic as Paul's question in Romans 10:14. If faith comes through hearing, how are they to hear without a preacher? God commands his word be spoken in sermons and made visible in sacraments. In the Augsburg Confession, Article 5 states:

> To obtain such faith God instituted the office of the ministry, that is, provided the Gospel and the sacraments. Through these, as through other means, God gives the Holy Spirit, who works faith, when and where he pleases, in those who hear the Gospel.

For Lutherans ordained ministry means proclamation of the Gospel rather than re-presentation of Christ.[18] The ordained minister is not a priest in a sacrificial ritual or a persuader urging a Christian view of life, but a proclaimer of the promises of Christ. Because ordained ministry means proclaiming the promises of Christ, then proclaimers of the promises cannot be restricted to those who are male, Jewish, or whatever. No accidents of birth, neither race nor sex, can disqualify one from ordination. Re-presentation is not the issue. What matters is delivering the message, the promises of Christ, "to you." As Luther wrote:

> For our faith and the sacrament must not be based on the person whether he is godly or evil, consecrated or unconsecrated, called or an impostor, whether he is the devil or his mother, but upon Christ, upon his word, upon his office, upon his command and ordinance; where these are in force, there everything will be carried out properly, no matter who or what the person might be.[19]

The Lutheran understanding of ministry is expressed with particular clarity in the final report of the eighth round of the U.S. Lutheran-Catholic dialogue: "Christ alone is the sole mediator and the one who is mediated."[20] More specifically, applied to our question, "the word and the sacraments are sometimes spoken of as 'means' (*Mittel, instrumenta*) through which the Holy Spirit gives faith to those who receive the gospel (CA5)."[21] Lutherans "rarely

speak of 'mediation' in this connection and prefer rather to speak
of the ministry of word and sacrament, the actual doing of the deed
in the living present."[22] Lutherans have refrained from extending the
category of the means of grace "through exemplary or properly
authorized 'intermediaries' " in such a way that "mediation (is extended) ecclesiologically via sacramental ordination, episcopacy, and
perhaps speaking of the church as sacrament here on earth. . . ."[23]

To sum it all up: the decision in 1970 to ordain women was
not traumatic for Lutherans largely because it did not involve fundamental change in their doctrine of ministry. Since the Augsburg
Confession of 1530, Lutherans have held that ordained ministry
means proclamation rather than re-presentation through a special
priesthood which stands *in persona Christi*. The office of ministry,
that is, the actual preaching of the word and sacraments, is divinely
ordained, even though ordained ministers, male or female, are not
in themselves instruments of salvation.[24]

THE CALL

When I first began to consider studying theology, I wondered
if I ought to "feel called." There was no lightning on the road to
Damascus for me; I just wanted to study theology. As college graduation neared, I spoke tentatively to the campus pastor about attending
seminary. He assured me that I did not need "to experience" a calling.
Indeed, all experience, including the experience of faith itself, is
ambiguous. In all decisions the only certainty we have is based on
God's faithfulness to his promises rather than a security based on
any experience, even a striking religious experience. Who is called
to the public ministry? The church, he said, extends the call.[25] His
advice: Go study, and let the church take care of the rest.

I did and I loved it – the courses, the professors, and the seminar
debates. No professor or student ever stated that women should not
be ordained or treated me disrespectfully. If anyone harbored doubts
about what I was doing there, it was me. I still was not sure about
ordination, but studying theology was exciting.[26]

Lutheran candidates for ordained ministry spend the third of
the four year seminary program in a congregation. I spent my internship year at an urban church in a transitional neighborhood in
Minneapolis. During that year I became convinced that if the church
called me to serve as a pastor, I would say "yes."

Six months after I graduated from the seminary and was certi-fied for call by the faculty and bishops, a suburban church outside Minneapolis called me to be an assistant pastor. Lutheran congrega-tions have a great deal to say about who holds the office of public ministry within and on behalf of the congregation: "The churches retain the right to ordain for themselves. For wherever the church exists, the right to administer the gospel also exists. Wherefore it is necessary for the church to retain the right of calling, electing and ordaining ministers."[27]

I was ordained in March 1979 without any intimation that the laying on of hands guaranteed that I would faithfully proclaim the Gospel or that I was endowed with special power for administrating the sacraments. Rather, my ordination conferred the authority to publicly proclaim the Gospel and administer the sacraments. For three years I regularly preached and administered the sacraments, taught confirmation and adult classes, visited shut-ins, and officiated at weddings and funerals.

Was I effective? When I preached, were many converted? These questions require a twofold answer. On the one hand, I always felt accepted by the vast majority of the people. Reservations about having a female pastor were seldom if ever voiced. Occasionally someone would say that the idea of a female pastor had been more unsettling than the reality. On the other hand, Lutherans teach that the Holy Spirit gives faith when and where it pleases God in those who hear the Gospel (Augsburg Confession, Article 5). Lutheran confessional documents protect against confusion concerning the working of the Holy Spirit. The Augsburg Confession, Article 8, acknowledges that while the Spirit through the Word creates faith, the power of the Word is not possessed by the church as a public institution – ". . . in this life many false Christians, hypocrites, and even open sinners remain among the godly. . . ."[28] Neither is the power of the Word possessed by its proclaimers – ". . .the sacraments are efficacious even if the priests who administer them are wicked men. . . ."[29] Nor does the efficacy of the Word depend on the wit and wisdom of the sermon. The power of the Gospel is not enhanced or diminished by human eloquence, for it is precisely in our fool-ishness (from the world's viewpoint) that the power of the cross, which is God's power, can be effective through the Holy Spirit (1 Cor. 1:17, 24-25). Thus the efficacy of my ministry is not something I control or can even measure. The efficacy of sermon and sacrament is guaranteed by Christ's promise alone.

OTHER MINISTRIES OPEN TO WOMEN

I temporarily resigned from public ministry after three years to be a full time wife and mother to our two small children. A year later, however, I accepted a part-time call to work as the ecumenical assistant to the bishop of the American Lutheran Church. For the next two years I had the unique opportunity of coordinating ecumenical events and informing the bishop of ecumenical developments. This work regularly brought me into contact with some of the best theologians of my tradition as well as of other traditions. Here again I was always treated with respect and courtesy, even by individuals who believed that women ought not be ordained.

I am currently finishing my doctorate in Reformation studies and raising our two children. In the future I would happily serve as a parish pastor, administrative staff, or teacher, depending on the situation. All positions in the Evangelical Lutheran Church in America are open to women, and women currently serve at all levels of our church. At the present two of the 66 bishops of our church are women, and worldwide there are seven Lutheran women bishops.

ECUMENICAL CONSEQUENCES

Wolfhart Pannenberg, a Lutheran Professor at Munich, Germany, has said "the greatest obstacle to ecumenism anywhere" is women's ordination.[30] If this is true, then perhaps for the sake of Christian unity, women ought not be ordained? After all, as Lutherans have said, ordaining women is not a *status confessionis* question for Lutherans, that is: binding for the faith. Lutherans may legitimately differ on this matter without the Gospel itself being at stake.[31] But is Pannenberg's statement true? Are women the greatest obstacle to unity? Even if Lutherans ordained only men, Lutheran orders would still be judged deficient by Anglican, Roman Catholic, and Orthodox churches. Basic differences on the question of ministry remain. The question of ordaining women is a secondary question that quickly leads to primary questions that have divided the churches for centuries: questions about the nature and purpose of ordained ministry, teaching authority, and the role of the church in salvation.

For example, in the Roman Catholic Church the question about women priests has been decisively addressed. Pope John Paul II has said there must be "no more discussion" of women priests. In his May 1994 Apostolic Letter, *Ordinatio Sacerdotalis*, the pope writes, "I declare that the Church has no authority whatsoever to confer priestly ordination on women and that this judgment is to be definitively held by all the Church's faithful."

In using the word "definitively," the Pope has upped the ante in matters of papal authority. According to some sources, he wanted to make this an infallible, *ex cathedra* declaration, but his more moderate advisors counseled against this.[32] He seems to have held that this was too important to leave to the ordinary magisterium and introduced a new category of teaching, "definitively," heretofore unknown in the terminology of papal teaching authority. It would seem that this declaration is not strictly infallible but more infallible than previous pronouncements on this question.[33]

Of course, even absolute papal statements have changed over the centuries, as numerous scholars have noted.[34] Already *Ordinatio Sacerdotalis* has been challenged. For example, the Belgian Catholic bishops responded to *Ordinatio Sacerdotalis* by calling for a broader discussion about tradition:

> Is tradition really the sole norm of faith, and if so what is the meaning of the Spirit's guidance? More generally, are there no new questions that have not been answered by tradition because they have not previously been asked?[35]

In spite of the Pope's definitive ruling there is much discussion and questioning among Catholic laity, priests, bishops, religious and theologians, as every reader of independent Catholic journals knows.

WHICH GOSPEL SHALL WE PREACH?

Pannenberg's claim that women's ordination is the greatest obstacle to ecumenism was made partly in response to the now-notorious "Re-Imagining" Conference held in Minneapolis, Minnesota, in November 1993. The question of ordaining women, according to Pannenberg, has grown in magnitude because the Vatican sees it as being linked to radical feminism. The linkage between the ordination of women and radical feminism is troublesome. To be sure, some women promote heretical doctrines as new feminist truths. The Re-Imagining Conference was widely criticized in the independent journals of mainline churches for promoting heretical doctrines.[36] Yet throughout church history the presence of male heretics has not caused the churches to consider refusing to ordain any men at all. So why should no woman be ordained just because some women are heretics? Nevertheless, many Lutheran women and men would agree with Pannenberg that radical feminism is "counterproductive to women's best interests in the church."[37]

Women, Lutheran or otherwise, do not agree upon what is in their best interests. Christina Hoff Sommers, a philosophy professor at Clark University in Worcester, Massachusetts, describes current divisions in secular feminism as a conflict between "equity" feminism and "gender" feminism.[38] Equity feminism is simply the belief in the moral and legal equality of the sexes. An equity feminist wants for women what she wants for everyone – a level playing field and equal opportunity. Gender feminism, on the other hand, is an all-encompassing ideology that says women are trapped in a patriarchal oppressive system and the only way out is by constructing new realities based on women's experience.

A similar fault line exists between Lutheran feminists. Lutheran equity feminists believe in and work for the equality of men and women in the church. This includes the ordination of women and their access to all levels of church leadership. At the same time equity feminists pledge themselves to the same confessional standards as do the men in their church: salvation is by faith alone, through grace alone, in Christ alone. These Lutheran women are not ashamed to hold that Christian faith and language are tied to historical particularity, to the life, death, and resurrection of Jesus, a first century male Jew.[39]

Lutheran gender feminists, by contrast, generally assert that Christianity is fatally flawed by patriarchal assumptions and must be fundamentally revised or "re-imagined" to reflect their own experience. In doing so, such feminist theologians abandon the particularity of the gospel and their theologies become a reflection of feminist consciousness. Not surprisingly, when experience has control and priority over revelation, then God reveals to you what you always wanted to hear. Theologians, including Lutheran feminist theologians, who grant hermeneutical weight to human experience implicitly challenge the Lutheran way of doing theology, which is to promote Christ alone (*was Christum treibet*).

In 1995, American Lutherans marked the twentieth-fifth anniversary of the ordination of women. The official ELCA celebration of this event is titled, "Breaking Open the Jar: 25 years of Remembrance and Hope." This three day event "honors the gifts of women" and generally focuses on women and their achievements. Among the objectives for the event, there is none which mentions the Gospel of Jesus Christ and only one activity – finding inclusive images for God – mentions the Lord whom women have been called to serve. Worship services will "emphasize contemplation," not the proclamation characteristic of the Lutheran tradition. Interest groups will focus primarily on relational questions – how women relate to male colleagues, laity, mobility in the church, and ministry and mothering. There are no interest groups raising questions about feminist theology from a Lutheran perspective or exploring the richness of the Lutheran doctrine of ministry. The program is focused on power and image issues and seems designed exclusively by Lutheran gender feminists.

The tone of this and other official celebrations of this anniversary prompted one female seminary professor to write the following:

> I am happy to join the church in celebrating (the 25th anniversary of the ordination of women). We should however, remember that wherever we find ourselves in the ministry of the church, our task is to proclaim Christ, and him crucified. There is no other reason for calling women into the ministry. For this reason, I am distressed to note that too many of the celebrations of this event seem to focus on the gifts women bring to the task of proclamation, rather than the joyful Gospel they are called to preach. In most of the publicity for the celebrations of this anniversary, there has been too little about our Lord and Savior Jesus Christ, and too much about women. This lack of witness to Jesus Christ would have mystified our foremothers, from Mary, the Mother of Our Lord, to the woman who broke open the alabaster jar, on down to the women missionaries of the last 150 years who could not stop telling of Jesus because of what he had done for them and could do for others by his death and resurrection. We should do no less.[40]

Other Lutheran women, like this professor, are challenging the leadership of Lutheran gender feminists. An ad-hoc group of ordained Lutheran women is hosting an independent celebration parallel to the official three day gathering. Calling themselves Daughters of the Word, they are offering a single evening event that focuses on the Lutheran understanding of ordination and celebrates the newfound wholeness of the church that has come through the inclusion of Lutheran women in ordained ministry.[41]

NOTES

1. Gracia Grindal, "Getting Women Ordained," *Called and Ordained: Lutheran Perspectives on the Office of the Ministry,* T. Nichol and M. Kolden, eds. (Minneapolis: Fortress Press, 1990) 161-79.

2. The first Lutheran church to permit the ordination of women was the Evangelical Lutheran Church in the Kingdom of the Netherlands, which introduced the possibility in 1922 and ordained a woman in 1928. In 1938 the Norwegian government granted the right to appoint women pastors if they were not rejected by the congregation. However, the first Norwegian woman was not ordained until 1961. Denmark permitted the ordination of women in 1947, Czechoslovakia in 1953, Sweden in 1959, France prior to 1962, and most of Germany by 1968. A survey conducted by the Lutheran World Federation in the early 1980s showed that over fifty Lutheran churches were ordaining women.

3. Grindal, *Called,* 173.

4. See Raymond Tiemeyer, *The Ordination of Women* (Minneapolis: Augsburg, 1970).

5. *D. Martin Luther's Werke* Kritische Gesamtausgabe (Weimar: Bohlau, 1883ff.) Tischreden 1:7 (hereinafter WA); *Luther's Works,* ed. by J. Pelikan, H.C. Oswald, and H. T. Lehmann, vols. 1-30 (St. Louis: Concordia Publishing House, 1955-86); vols. 31-55 (Philadelphia: Fortress Press, 1957-86) 54:8 (hereinafter LW).

6. Cited by Steven Ozment, *The Age of Reform* (New Haven: Yale University Press, 1980) 383.

7. WA 12:308; LW 30:55.

8. Cf. WA Tischreden 2: #2580.

9. WA 12:185; LW 40:23,25.

10. WA 8:489, 497-98, LW 36:141, 151:52; WA 12:180:81, LW 40:23; WA 12:722, LW 35:18; WA 30:111, LW 51:183; WA 30:524, LW 46:220; WA 50:633, LW 41:158.

11. WA 12:18; LW 40:23.

12. WA 6:501; LW 36:18, cf. Melanchthon in Apology 13:4, p. 211 in *The Book of Concord: The Confessions of the Evangelical Lutheran Church,* Theodore G. Tappert, ed. and tr. (Philadelphia: Fortress Press, 1958.)

13. "Women in the Church: Scriptural Principles and Ecclesial Practice," *A Report of the Commission on Theology and Church Relations of The Lutheran Church – Missouri Synod* (September, 1985).

14. The 1976 *Declaration on the Question of the Admission of Women to the Ministerial Priesthood (Inter insigniores)* issued by the Congregation for the Doctrine of the Faith has set forth the Roman Catholic position that only males can be ordained because only males can represent Christ, a male. In his letter of February 17, 1986, to Archbishop Runcie, Cardinal Willebrands, using *Inter insigniores,* states:

> The ordination only of men to the priesthood has to be understood in terms of the intimate relationship between Christ the redeemer and those who, in a unique way, cooperate in Christ's redemptive work. The priest represents Christ in his saving relationship with his body the church.

On May 30, 1994, Pope John Paul II issued an apostolic letter, *Ordinatio Sacerdotalis,* reaffirming the Catholic Church's ban on women priests. He emphasizes that the disciples were specifically and intimately associated with Christ's mission and that their apostolic mission is to represent Christ. Specifically it is in the sacrifice of the Mass that the priest is intimately associated with Christ: "For it is one and the same victim: he who now makes the offering through the ministry of priests and he who then offered himself on the cross; the only difference is in the manner of the offering."

15. Efforts to minimize the offense of the gospel are not new. In the 1930s some German Christians were offended by Jesus' Jewishness, so they revised the Bible to minimize his Jewishness. In a similar way some feminists today take offense at the fact that Jesus was a man and therefore they revise the Bible to minimize his maleness. Such efforts are problematic. The Christian faith has to do with revelation in time, through historical particularity. God came in the flesh in the first century as a Jewish man, probably about 5'7" with a hooked nose. Efforts to minimize some aspect of Jesus' person in order to conform to modern sensibilities inevitably leads to a Gnostic distortion of the gospel.

16. WA 10/2:282; LW 45:24.

17. See Roy Harrisville, "Ministry in the New Testament," *Called and Ordained,* T. Nichol and M. Kolden, eds. (Minneapolis: Augsburg, 1990) 3-23, for a standard Lutheran interpretation of the New Testament witness on this question.

18. *Ministry, Women, Bishops: Report of an International Consultation in Cartigny, Switzerland 1992.* The Lutheran World Federation (Geneva: LWF, 1993). Although this document has a certain status as a Lutheran World Federation report, it does not develop a Lutheran argument: it does not proceed methodologically from the Word, as can be seen especially in its discussion of adiaphora pp. 30-31 and "The Lutheran Concept of Pastoral Ministry," pp. 66-67.

19. WA 38:242; LW 38:200.

20. "Lutheran Perspectives on Critical Issues," *The One Mediator, The Saints, and Mary, Lutherans and Catholics in Dialogue,* eds. H. G. Anderson J. F. Stafford, J. A. Burgess (Minneapolis: Augsburg, 1992), p. 38.

21. *The One Mediator,* 38.

22. *The One Mediator,* 38.

23. *The One Mediator,* 39.

24. Walter Kasper, "Basic Consensus and Church Fellowship," *In Search of Christian Unity* (Minneapolis: Augsburg, 1991) 36: "In Catholic understanding the sacramentality of the church means not only that the church is the place and sign of salvation, but also that it is the instrument of salvation. As a matter of comparison, the document on doctrinal condemnations in the sixteenth century notes that Protestant doctrine also holds that 'mediation' of the doctrine of justification happens in the church, but Protestants have reservations about speaking of 'mediation' through the church."

25. For Lutherans, entrance into the public ministry is on the basis of a properly or regularly agreed upon manner, as stated in Augsburg Confession, Article 14: "It is taught among us that nobody should publicly teach or preach or administer the sacraments in the church without a regular call."

26. Of the 130 Master of Divinity students in my class six were women. In 1994-95 there were 725 women preparing for ordination in the eight seminaries of the Evangelical Lutheran Church in America, 44.8% of total enrollment.

27. *Treatise on the Power and Primacy of the Pope*, 67, in Tappert, *The Book of Concord.*

28. *Book of Concord*, p. 33.

29. *Book of Concord*, p. 33.

30. *National Christian Reporter*, May 27, 1994.

31. The Lutheran Church of Latvia revoked the ordination of women in 1995.

32. Tom Fox, "Bishops pull pope back from brink," *National Catholic Reporter*, June 17, 1994, p. 3.

33. Now that it is clear that "definitively" equals "infallibly," future discussions of women's ordination *both* for Roman Catholics and Lutherans should focus on teaching authority. Roman Catholics should not be sidetracked by the fact that, in the ebb and flow of Vatican diplomacy, women will soon be ordained to the permanent diaconate, and Lutherans should not be sidetracked by the success or failure of radical feminism in our culture."

34. Peter Hebblethwaite, "Ban on women priests is shaky conclusion," *National Catholic Reporter*, September 2, 1994, p. 12.

35. Peter Hebblethwaite, "Catholics try to digest papal bombshell," *National Catholic Reporter*, July 1, 1994, p. 6.

36. For a Lutheran critique see Katherine Kersten, "God in Your Mirror?" and "Old Heresies from New Feminists," *Lutheran Commentator*, vol. 7, no. 6 (May/June 1994).

37. *National Christian Reporter*, May 27, 1994.

38. Christina Hoff Summers, *Who Stole Feminism: How Women Have Betrayed Women* (New York: Simon & Schuster, 1994).

39. Gerhard Forde, "Naming the One Who is Above Us," *Speaking the Christian God*, A. F. Kimel, Jr., ed. (Grand Rapids: Eerdmans, 1992), pp. 110-19.

40. Gracia Grindal, "25th Celebration: too little about Jesus, too much about women," *The Concord*, 27 (April 6, 1995) p. 8.

41. A recent survey conducted by the Student Resource Center of the largest Lutheran seminary in the U.S. found that "the overwhelming majority (of women) have reported satisfaction with their decisions to become pastors." See "Resource Center surveys women alumnae," *The Concord*, 27, no. 13 (1995) p. 1.

4

"You Sure Did Look Like an Angel!"

Rev. Jeanne Marechal

The maple tree outside the parsonage window is finally in full leaf. I've been watching its seasonal evolution during my weekly sermon preparations. I find it strangely reassuring to put my thoughts together at the kitchen table while looking out at this tree. On those days when thoughts are hard to come by and the Spirit seems to be busy elsewhere, this old, ever-changing tree serves as a gentle reminder of God's constant presence and dependability.

Tomorrow's sermon is finished – finally. It is a good sermon. No! Good is not the right word; it is a faithful sermon. Over the years I have come to the conclusion that there is no such thing as a "good" sermon or even a "bad" one – although I'm very aware others might dispute this claim (and on occasion I've even heard a few that tempt me to rescind this statement). As preacher, my responsibility is to proclaim the Word of God as faithfully as I am able. How the Word is received I have learned to leave in God's hands. This lesson has not been an easy one for me to learn. After seventeen years of preaching, I am still amazed at the impact my sermons may or may not have on my congregation. How often the messages I thought to be my best receive absolutely no response, while those I am most concerned about, the least confident of, touch someone deeply. Perhaps it is God's way of reminding me again and again of who really is in charge and whose Word is proclaimed!

Does God's involvement give me permission to work less, plan less, think less in my preparation? Absolutely not! However, it does allow me to be less self-reliant, less self-conscious, less compulsive about what I am called to do and be. I did not always feel this way; this mode of thinking has been an evolutionary process for me.

As a student, I agonized over my first sermon, trying as hard as I could to be meaningful, insightful, diligent and . . . profound. I was the first female seminary student to serve this large, metropolitan church in Chicago, and I felt every ounce of that burden of responsibility. I was nervous, but I knew that I was also well prepared, well read, well rehearsed. After that worship service, an elderly gentleman shook my hand, looked me in the eye, and very sincerely offered, "I don't know what you said up there, honey, but you sure did look like an angel!"

Soon after that experience, I traded in my white alb for a black liturgical robe and stopped wearing make-up. My long hair I parted in the middle and, at least on Sundays, wore pulled back in a tight knot at the base of my neck. If I could have seen through eyeglasses, I would have purchased a pair of those, too. I was a *minister* and I desperately wanted to be acknowledged as authentic – and to be taken seriously. I was determined that the fact that I was an attractive woman would not hamper that identification or my authenticity in any way. (In my indignation, I forgot that most of the biblical angels were male so it was a lousy analogy in the first place!)

Fortunately, my severe and solemn period did not last very long. With the guidance of some key professors and reflection with seminary peers, I soon made several important discoveries. Initially, I believed that many of the difficulties I was encountering were gender specific. Much to my surprise, I found that a number of the male students – usually those who were young and attractive – were encountering the same difficulties in being taken seriously. They felt patronized, especially by the older women in their congregations who either made passes at them or wanted to take them home and feed them!

I also learned that it was not unusual for congregations to feel ambivalence toward their students. After all, it is the Senior Minister who *really* represents the church! (This problem of authenticity exists in many congregations for Associate Ministers as well, e.g., "It's nice that she visits me, but when is the *real* minister going to make a call?")

Another critical discovery for me was understanding that in order to be authentic I needed to be as true as possible to who *I* am. I needed to have faith that God called me into ministry knowing exactly who I am and wanting me just the same. What a humbling and reassuring revelation!

I began to understand then, that God calls many kinds of people into ministry. Some who have brilliant minds and some who are barely able to think through the day; some who have great physical attractiveness and some who have little outward beauty but gorgeous hearts; some who can speak well and some who can write well; some who have strong pastoral presence and some whose strength is in administration; some who look the part of a minister and many who don't fit any projected mold whatsoever! Apparently, human perceptions of clergy are quite different from God's! So, too, are their expectations.

I find that two of the greatest difficulties in ministry are resisting the temptation to live up to the expectations of others and recognizing how unreasonable and unattainable those expectations usually are. It has taken me years to be able to say with conviction that I am not, never have been and never will be the person that some are looking for in their pastor (though I must admit that at times I still am tempted to try and meet those expectations). I have finally come to own in my heart what I have long known in my head: I simply cannot be all things to all people. No one can. With this understanding has come a second important realization: my ministry for God is seriously compromised when my personal need for approval becomes a primary goal.

At times the dissatisfaction with my ministry is obvious – as in the fact that I cannot be a male pastor or that I am not a theological conservative. At other times, the dissatisfaction is quite covert and takes considerable foraging to uncover. A former parishioner of mine was critical of nearly everything I did or said. She found fault with my sermons, with my worship leadership style and with my administrative techniques. If I made suggestions, she accused me of being authoritarian; if I encouraged lay leadership, she accused me of being negligent in my pastoral responsibilities. I could not please this woman no matter how hard I tried! A long time later, I discovered the true reason for her animosity: she had once been terribly wounded by a former friend who bore a great physical resemblance to me. The good news is that we were able to reconcile our relationship. She was no longer my adversary, though she never became my friend. It would be unrealistic of me to expect more. Trust, respect and approval are not commodities that are automatically conferred with the title "Reverend."

Regardless of logic or rationalization, criticism still hurts. Criticism especially hurts after an eighty-hour work week and an all-out effort to be faithful and conscientious. Sometimes it seems as if everyone knocking at my door comes to name a personal failure of mine. Yet, through these most discouraging moments I have learned another valuable lesson: one of the most important tools of ministry is a clear sense of self – of gifts and of flaws, of strengths and weaknesses both. Without this self-awareness, the temptation to succumb to the projections of others becomes almost undefendable. This surrender produces devastating results either in the forms of wavering insecurity and timidity or pompous rigidity and authoritarianism. Both of these are defensive overreactions which I need to avoid at all costs, for my own health and the health of my congregation.

Practically speaking, I have found in each congregation I've served, some people who think I can do no wrong and some people who think I can do no right. Luckily, only a few are found at these extremes. The vast majority of congregants fall somewhere in the middle of this continuum and have a fairly healthy understanding of human limitations and frailty. Best of all, they carry an immense capacity for forgiveness. I remind myself of these attributes often because God's call to minister the Children of the Promise is as difficult and demanding as it is fulfilling and satisfying.

I had not planned to be a minister. In fact, I don't recall ever considering ministry in even the most remote way! Science was my forte; becoming a surgeon was my goal. How terribly disappointed I was when that dream did not materialize! And then, suddenly, unexpectedly, vehemently, God grabbed me by the shoulders, turned me around and pointed me in a new direction. I understood what people meant when they referred to ministry as a "call." I entered Chicago Theological Seminary six months later as a pregnant, second-career woman in my mid-thirties, confident that I was in the right place but much less sure about where I was headed or how I was to get there. (Faith is a key word in many ways!)

My close friends and professors were enthusiastically supportive of my pursuits, as were my husband and three-year-old daughter. When our son was born in January, he attended many of my classes in a small wicker basket which I kept at my feet. I interpreted his quiet cooperation as support as well!

With strangers and acquaintances, however, response to my decision to enter seminary ran the gamut from awe and amazement to genuine confusion and surprise bordering on shock ("What's a nice girl like you doing in a profession like that?!!"). Perhaps the most uncomfortable situations during those early years were social gatherings. When I was asked in conversation what I did for a living, the reaction to my response that I was in seminary usually came in one of two forms. People became noticeably uncomfortable, began shifting their weight, and proceeded to confess why they no longer attended church. Then they tried as quickly and politely as possible to escape my presence. These people also tended to avoid me for the rest of the evening – in one instance going so far as to rearrange place cards on the dinner tables!

The second form of reaction was almost exactly the opposite. Some people became incredibly fascinated with the prospect of me as a woman minister and I was inundated with questions (often personal and inappropriate) or with theological inquiries and challenges that I could not have begun to answer even if I had wanted to! In those cases it was I who tried as quickly and politely as possible to escape their presence. Cocktail parties, as you can imagine, were particularly disastrous!

While my social adventures as a minister-in-training were often awkward, my professional student ministry was a time of discovery and assimilation, of establishing the root system that would support my future ministry. It was a time not only to gather the basic academic knowledge and clinical practice necessary for parish ministry, but also to discover who I was and how I fit into God's plan. It was a challenging time, but looking back I see that it was also a safe time. I was surrounded by people – professors, field education supervisors, academic advisors and peers – whose primary goals were to help me shape my ministry. It was a time to try new things and to make mistakes, all with the knowledge that I was protected by the strong safety net of the seminary community if I should fall or fail.

My first official call was as "Minister of Congregational Life and Small Group Development," otherwise known as part-time associate pastor. It was a perfect position for me! My family had moved to a suburb north of Chicago and the calling church was located literally down the street from where we lived. My third child was born the year after I graduated from CTS, and his nursery school was located across the street from the church. My husband traveled frequently and so the twenty-hour-a-week position allowed me time to uphold my family responsibilities as well.

This associate position offered me the opportunity not only for ordination, but also for more personal growth. Up to this point, I had only observed the sacramental aspects of church life. In this new position, I had the opportunity to participate regularly in serving communion and to officiate at baptisms, weddings and funerals. Yet, this environment was a protected one as well. While I certainly had designated responsibilities for some areas of church life, I was sheltered from the full load of pastoral leadership: administrative responsibilities, weekly sermon preparations, etc. And, because I was the associate and not the senior pastor, I was also sheltered from much of the criticism and complaints that were taken to the *real* ministers who had the authority to do something about them! After nearly three years in this position I felt that I had accomplished those promises which I had been called to fulfill: several small groups were established and functioning well on their own; two pastoral care teams were trained and on track; the women's group had been reactivated; and an intergenerational dinner program had been established that was always well attended. The senior co-pastors were away for six weeks each summer, and for three years during their absence, I was "in charge," The first year, I was anxious to see them return! The second year, I felt that I was just settling into my rhythm when they came back and I wished their time away was twice as long! By the end of the third summer, I longed to spread my wings and fly on my own. I knew I would not be content to remain in that particular position much longer and so I began to search for a church of my own.

During the summer of 1988, I was called as sole pastor to a small, suburban UCC church in New England. This particular community was largely Roman Catholic with little or no experience of female pastoral leadership. It was during this phase of my ministry that I encountered some interesting situations because I was an ordained woman.

For the first time since ordination I came up against confusion about my title. I was referred to as many things by those who were unfamiliar with women ministers: "priestess," "Madam Reverend," and "Mother Marechal" were perhaps the most common. On more than one occasion I had to shout and demand attention during boisterous wedding rehearsals because most of the wedding party believed me to be the wedding consultant rather than the attending pastor. ("Hey, cool!" was and still is the most common response to my real identity! Linguistically we move on from there, but at least it is an opening for possible new awareness!) I have had to explain that Yes! I do wear a robe when I do a baptism or a wedding, but No! I do not wear one all the time, nor do I wear a collar to bed or in the shower. Obviously patience and a sense of humor are indispensable ministerial assets!

The move from part-time associate to full-time pastor was traumatic! Weekly preaching responsibilities were much greater than I ever imagined! It was here that I got caught (and caught good) trying to be all things to all people. In my previous position, parishioners had rarely come to me with concerns or complaints. Now it seemed as though I spent an extraordinary amount of time putting out "brush fires" and addressing complaints. I tried harder and harder to meet all of the needs expressed; exerting more and more energy; spending more and more time working; and becoming more and more disillusioned about both my call and my gifts.

Yet it was in this placement that I learned how to preach, how to pastor, how to listen compassionately and how to pray! I learned to name my weaknesses as well as my gifts. It was here that I felt God's loving presence surround the bedside of the dying, beautiful nine-year-old daughter of one of my parishioners. It was here that an old woman held out her hands to me and prayed for me and my ministry after I had prayed for her. It was in this church that I comprehended God's great commandment to love one another – even those people whom I didn't like, let alone want to love!

As I was learning to juggle family, church and personal needs, I also learned to gift myself. Wednesday-evening art classes became a priority on my weekly agenda. It was a time to remove myself from everything else that pulled and tugged and yanked at me all week long. It was time to clear my mind, to renew and refresh myself. It was the gift of a lifetime!

My family was not immune from confusion and misconceptions about women in ministry either. My husband was actually invited to several women's functions because the previous ministers' wives had always attended. No one quite knew what to do with him, but they did not want him to feel excluded. He, too, has been addressed as many things, from Mr. Jeanne Marechal to being called Reverend himself.

My daughter remembers arguing with a high school teacher about a form she filled out which listed her "Mother's profession" as minister. The form was returned to her for correction.

"You mean your father is a minister."

"No, my mother!"

"Your mother can't be a minister, she's a woman. It must be your father!"

"No! It's my mother, not my father! Don't you think I know the difference between my mother and my father?!"

I believe Kate received a detention for insubordination which she was none too pleased about. After that incident, however, she took great pride in the fact her mother was such an oddity in the community and used every opportunity to point out her mother's called profession!

My daughter was not the only one who was misunderstood. The older of my sons quit scouting in the middle of the fourth grade when one of the leaders responded to his antics with, "I certainly never expected that kind of behavior from you of all people, considering what your mother does for a living!" That was the end of Boy Scouts for Drew and the beginning of a whole new behavior pattern designed to offset any preconceived notions about how a minister's son should behave. On the whole, many people still view the minister's children with certain behavioral expectations that are difficult for them to live up to. It is often a heavy cross for them to bear.

Today, I occasionally encounter parishioners who appear to have problems with the fact that I am a woman pastor. On deeper inquiry, however, nearly all of these people, men or women, have other issues at the root of their dissatisfaction. Usually these people may be unable either to recognize or articulate the real issues (as in the case of the woman mentioned earlier), or they are people who may have problems with authority figures of any kind. While opposition to my ministry may appear to be gender based, I am convinced that if I were a male pastor, the opposition would still be there – it would just surface in another way.

The larger issue of my Ecclesiastical "right" to be ordained and to administer the sacraments is not of particular significance for me although I realize so many other women still face this issue daily. I am blessed in the fact that while women in ministry are still not "the norm," the United Church of Christ strongly supports and affirms the ordination of women and has for several generations. Most of the UCC discussions involving a woman's right to ordination took place many years ago, and I realize that I have only to thank those men and women who have gone before me and smoothed the way.

Here I offer a word of hope and encouragement to my sisters in ministry still struggling with issues similar to those my denomination faced in the '70s. I believe that people of faith who *are* the Church, the ones in the pews as opposed to those in the political hierarchy, are remarkably flexible and open to new ways that God's voice may be heard in the wilderness of our lives. I also have found that the vast majority of parishioners acknowledge the fact that gender does not ensure incompetence in any field of endeavor any more than it ensures excellence – and that includes ministry! In my experience, many of the people who were initially the most hesitant about my leadership because of my being a woman have become very ardent supporters, not just of me personally, but of the whole concept of women in ministry. Oftentimes, I believe that acceptance is a matter of exposure as much as anything else. In the UCC, women are often recommended for Interim Ministry in churches that have had no experience of female leadership. It has been interesting for me to note the number of these churches that then go on to call a woman for their permanent pastoral position.

I have had people join the church *because* I am a woman pastor, and I have lost congregants for exactly the same reason. But to the vast majority of my parishioners – both past and present, both male and female – I do not believe that gender plays a significant role in my ministry. Several years ago, a woman from a neighboring town began attending worship with us. She was always alone. After nearly six months of faithful attendance, she announced that she was going to bring her husband to church the next Sunday. She was pleased he had agreed to come for he had had a "bad" church experience and was extremely wary of the formal church. I did not have an opportunity to speak with them after worship, other than the perfunctory handshake and greeting since they left very quickly. I received a call from the woman the next day telling me about her husband's reaction: he liked the worship service, he found the sermon interesting and evocative, the other parishioners friendly and the music fantastic. He was perplexed about one thing, however: "Why didn't you tell me the minister was a woman? In all the time you've been attending that church, you never mentioned you had a woman pastor!"

The woman laughed as she relayed this conversation to me. She said, "It never even occurred to me to tell him that you were a woman. By the time I was halfway through that first worship service, I stopped thinking about the fact that you were a woman and I guess I've never thought about it again. You are my pastor; that's how I think of you. The fact that you are a woman just isn't significant to me."

How often I remember that conversation when I'm feeling down! What a great gift this woman gave me – so innocently and so freely. It would never occur to most people to identify their pastor as male. Isn't it wonderful that there are also people who have no need to identify their pastor as female?!

Outside, beyond the maple tree, I hear the voices of my two younger children playing tennis in the church parking lot. They are trying to teach our dog to retrieve the missed balls. But he is a retriever in name only – and is intent on catching all balls at first bounce and running as fast as possible with them in the opposite direction. Both boys are united in their efforts at this time, certainly not always the case with thirteen- and sixteen-year-old siblings. I listen to my children's laughter, and it makes me smile. I am confident that I am where God wants me to be.

We moved to this community two-and-one-half years ago where I am serving as Senior Pastor in the fifth church on my journey. My ministry here is strong, affirmed and supported by a loving, faithful congregation which has a long history of lay leadership and personal investment in the church. I am the first full-time pastor to serve this church in 27 years – and the first woman. It is a challenging opportunity, for this church is undergoing great change and change is never easy. Our membership has nearly doubled within the past five years and our church school has quadrupled. Two summers ago, major renovations added six new classrooms to our church school; this fall we will hold classes in the parsonage as well. To address increasing church school needs, a Minister of Christian Education was called and ordained in our church this past spring. She is a blessing to us all! (Now the church has to deal with not one, but two ordained women!)

Assimilation of new members into the life of the congregation is not something that can be taken for granted but must be carefully and conscientiously orchestrated. I sense that most of these new people are seekers. They are looking for meaning in their own lives and the lives of their children; they are looking for faith; they are looking for community; they are not specifically looking for a male pastor.

The issues I face as pastor involve so many different areas: financial support; assimilation of new members without alienating those that have been here for a long time; program development to meet the needs of the congregation; pastoral care and visitation; education and faith development; and striking a balance between the prophetic voice and pastoral reassurance . . . and the list goes on.

Nevertheless, I maintain that the issues I face as a UCC pastor in the '90s are not particularly gender related. The challenges I share with my colleagues are about authority, power, stewardship, communication, vision and faith; they are the same struggles as those of my male counterparts. I know this to be true because much of my own evolution as a minister has come as a result of reflection and conversation with others on the same journey.

The struggle for personal growth both as an individual and as a pastor never ceases. As with any profession, but I think especially with ours, we are called not only into covenant but also into communion with others. It is in the sharing of our stories with one another and in the blending of these stories with the timeless stories of God's grace and faithfulness, that our faith becomes more firmly rooted, change is nurtured and growth happens. As ministers, it is all too easy to isolate ourselves in our parishes, stoically going about our business of answering God's call. I have spoken with many clergy who feel caught between the need for supportive friendships and the isolation from peers that is often inherent to parish ministry.

Not only is collegial support personally helpful, but I believe that it is also critically important to our ministry. Time with trusted colleagues offers an opportunity for reflection and objective input. It is a time to give and receive encouragement, to exchange ideas, to face challenges, and to put parish concerns into perspective. The stinging criticism of unhappy parishioners can erode self-confidence and undermine a healthy ministry if it remains unchecked. Conversely, too comfortable of a situation can lead to complacency and laziness if it remains unchallenged. Without reflection and feedback, obstacles placed in our paths as women – ordination, appointments or calls to positions of leadership, and misconceptions about women in ministry – can appear insurmountable. The inevitable mistakes that we all make can take on gigantic proportions.

Faithful ministry is not an easy task; alone, it becomes nearly an impossibility. A supportive group of colleagues cannot eliminate all of the difficulties we may encounter, but it can help immeasurably in gaining perspective and charting a course for the future.

I hope that women still struggling will find it reassuring to know that many men, ordained as well as lay, support the ordination of women. Their voices need to be heard as well as ours, for God calls us both. I hope it is reassuring as well to know that at least in some churches the question of gender is not a significant issue any longer. With each passing day, I believe we are moving toward oneness in mission and away from the oppression of human biases.

It is night now and my children have long since stopped playing tennis and have come indoors. I cannot see the maple tree, but I know it is still outside my kitchen window – growing and changing, even in the dark. I trust that this old tree will be visible once again in the light of day.

In spite of my own occasional doubts and fears, I have experienced God's Spirit move through my life as I have made my responsive journey. I trust implicitly that God will continue to guide me in the future.

I end now with this blessing; it is one many of my congregants know by heart; it is both charge and benediction to us all:

Go now into the world in peace.
Be of good courage and hold fast to that which is good.
Render to no one evil for evil.
Strengthen the faint-hearted.
Support the weak.
Honor all people.
Love and serve God,
Rejoicing in the power that is given to you in the Holy Spirit.

Amen and Amen.

5

My Calling into the Pastoral Ministry

Rev. Elva Martin

In August 1985, my husband and I visited Gatlinburg, Tennessee, a mountain resort, for a brief, late summer vacation. Two years earlier, at forty, I had resigned my teaching career with the idea of going into full-time Christian writing. But two years into free-lance writing, I found myself battling the feeling that something was wrong or missing, dreadfully missing, in my life.

There in Gatlinburg early one morning I was awakened from a deep sleep with a sense of urgency to get alone and pray. Since my husband was a late sleeper, I dressed very quietly, picked up my purse, Bible and prayer journal and headed out of the hotel in the early morning sunshine. Just across the street from our hotel, the red door of a small church beckoned to me.

Somewhere in the back of my mind I recalled reading that this particular type of church left its door open for visitors or those who might want to come in and pray. I wondered if it were true. It would be a great place to pray.

I walked across the street and tried the door. It opened easily to my touch and I entered a lovely little sanctuary. The old-fashioned wooden pews were dark, unpadded and straight-backed but the rainbow-colored sunshine cascading over them through the stained glass windows issued an invitation. I saw no one about, and without further thought, I made my way to a middle row and sat down in a ray of sunlight.

The moment I sat down, I found myself in a sweet sense of God's presence. Praises and prayer came spontaneously to my lips.

After sometime I was reminded of the Bible in my lap. I opened it and felt led to 2 Timothy 4. My eyes read the words, but I was conscious of a voice deep in my spirit, personalizing them, engraving them on my heart. And it was like coming home after a long journey.

> I charge you in the presence of God and of Christ Jesus, Who is to judge the living and the dead, and by the light of His coming and His kingdom: herald and preach the Word! Keep your sense of urgency (stand by, be at hand and ready) whether the opportunity seems to be favorable or unfavorable. (Whether it is convenient or inconvenient, whether it is welcome or unwelcome, you as preacher of the Word are to show people in what ways their lives are wrong.) And convince them, rebuking and correcting, warning and urging and encouraging them, being unflagging and inexhaustible in patience and teaching." (2 Timothy 4:1-2, *Amplified Bible*)

I was astounded at the implication of these words but that Voice was so strong in my spirit and brought such a sense of peace, there was no room to doubt that God was indeed calling me into the ministry. At that time, He also reminded me He had first called me at age fourteen. For sometime I had been on the backside of the desert!

I remembered His call at age fourteen. At that time I was in a church that did not recognize women in ministerial roles. I talked to my pastor about the call I was feeling. He seemed to think I must be called into mission work and he suggested I pursue that idea. But I didn't feel led to pursue missions. Having no role models of women in any other kind of full-time ministry, I lost sight of the vision and upon graduation from high school I pursued a teaching degree with a minor in business. I worked in business for a time, then entered the teaching profession. During this time I was very active in my local church and held a number of leadership roles that were open to women from Children's Church Director to Women's Ministry Director to Junior Choir Leader.

But God had not released me from His call! He reminded me of this as I sat in that little chapel in Gatlinburg. Finally, I had an explanation for the feeling of loss, of not being in the center of God's will, that I had experienced for years! I also saw, coming from my background with no encouragement to follow God's call, how necessary it was for me to receive what the Pentecostals call "the baptism in the Holy Spirit" before I could really hear and follow God's call.

The Holy Spirit is the strongest Encourager of all. I received the baptism in the Holy Spirit at a meeting of Women's Aglow, an interdenominational Charismatic organization.

That morning in the Gatlinburg chapel, with the confidence only the Holy Spirit can give, I accepted God's call into the ministry. At that time I also asked God to put role models of women in the ministry in my path. I could see God's call in the scriptures, but I needed to see live role models of women answering that call.

God answered this prayer over the next couple of years, using my writing ability to open doors to interview and write articles on several women in ministry roles.

One of the ordained women he put in my path was Pastor Anne Jimenez of Rock Church in Virginia Beach. I saw in her example what God could do with a woman who fully yielded to His call and purposes. *Charisma Magazine* sent me to interview her and her husband John, who co-pastors with her, for the magazine's "Most Outstanding Churches of America" series.

Anne and I also talked about women's roles in ministry. She told me she believed women, coming into full ministry roles, were God's "secret weapon" for our endtimes. Her testimony as a young unmarried woman when she first shared her calling with her father should have prepared me for adverse responses to my calling. The night Anne shared her call into the ministry with her father, she had to leave her home with nothing but her car keys and purse. (Today both Anne's parents are in her church and have supported her ministry for years.)

I finally had peace with God about my calling after the Gatlinburg trip, but I found little peace from my husband and teenage son when I tried to share it with them. My husband, after failing to discourage me, warned me privately he would consider divorce if I pursued my calling.

My son said plainly one day, "Mother, if you ever put Reverend in front of your name, forget I am your son." My father was flabbergasted that I would even consider the idea.

At this time we had come out of our former denomination and into the Assemblies of God after my husband also received the baptism in the Holy Spirit. The Assemblies of God fully recognize women in all types of ministry roles. But it took a little time for my husband (and son) to cast aside the tradition about women's roles in ministry that our former denomination held. I prayed a lot and I had some conversations with my new pastor, Rick Collins, about what God was calling me to do. He encouraged me to follow God's call and had a large impact on my formation as a minister. His acceptance and encouragement of my calling also greatly helped my husband and son accept my calling, as did being in a denomination that fully recognized women in all types of ministry roles.

In 1986 I spearheaded a large interdenominational meeting in our city with several other speakers. After that meeting I began to hold monthly Bible Seminars in local rented halls. People came, received Christ and the baptism in the Holy Spirit and healing. God blessed in these meetings. I formed an evangelistic association and brought my ministry under a Board of Advisors.

My pastor also advised me to pursue credentials with the Assemblies of God. I fulfilled the Assemblies requirements and additional study and obtained credentials in January 1988.

In October of that same year God spoke to my heart to pioneer a new assembly in our city. To become a pastor was yet another big step of faith for me, even though our Assembly of God denomination fully endorsed women as pastors. I spent three days fasting and praying.

During that time I laid out before God all my doubts and fears. I even wrote them down in my prayer journal – my being a woman, my husband not being called to preach, although he is an excellent musician; my talking too fast; my lack of experience in pastoring; and, although people had accepted my teaching ministry, would they accept me in a pastoral role? God swooped right through my list, turned it topsy-turvy by answering in my spirit, "Count your assets as your liabilities and your liabilities as your assets."

We held prayer meetings in our home for four months, then opened the doors of Word of Truth Assembly in a shopping center on Easter Sunday, March 26, 1989. I pastor the church and my husband, Dwayne, is Minister of Music. We have currently purchased property and are entering our first building program.

In the six years of our pastoral ministry at Word of Truth we have experienced a number of blessings. For example, over 200 people are listed in our records as having made a profession of faith in Jesus Christ as Lord and Savior. We have seen marriages put back together. The first marriage ceremony I performed was between a man and woman who had divorced over a year earlier due in large part to his alcoholism. We saw God deliver this man from his alcoholism and then put this marriage back together. We have seen God perform miracles of physical heating. We have seen the spiritual growth of those who attend and we have experienced some financial blessings; such as, in 1994, when we were trying to purchase property, someone (not a member of our church) came to us, said they believed in our ministry and church, and handed us a check for $40,000.

Our church is also a place where different races and classes worship and work together, regardless of being in the Deep South.

Along with the blessings, we have struggled with some battles, a number of which any new work probably experiences: a lack of trained leadership, a revolving front door, a lack of commitment and not being able to get into discipleship all those who make professions of faith.

On the home front, my husband and I struggled over my role of authority in the church and how it related to home. But the Bible is clear on the fact that the Christian husband is head of the home. Relief came as we both learned to discern and draw lines between his authority over the home versus my authority over the church as its pastor. I laugh when I remember, but God really helped this process along even with the telephone. When hurting people called for pastoral help, you wouldn't believe how fast my husband learned to hand the phone to me! And I had to learn to take off my "pastor" hat at home and just be "wife," "mother," "chief cook and bottle-washer!" None of which is very anointed but is very satisfying! I would be happy to have my husband in a co-pastor position with me, but he is not called to that. He is called to music as strongly as I am called to pastoral ministry. And both calls complement each other. Our District Superintendent has been a great help in helping my husband and me honor, respect and complement each other's roles.

In the future I see more pastoral roles for women opening up in the Christian community. Why? Because the task is too great, the laborers too few, to exclude any truly-called, qualified and dedicated laborers due simply to gender. Paul said in Galatians 3:28: There is neither Jew nor Greek, slave nor free, male nor female, for you are all one in Christ. Racial barriers, class barriers, gender barriers are cast down in Christ. I believe this applies to the laborers as well as to the white fields of harvest.

A great reconciliation is taking place in the Body of Christ and it is in all three of these areas. Government will never be able to implement by law what God wants to implement by love. I believe much of the Church today is beginning to see this and true reconciliation is coming.

Personally, I still view with love those in the Christian community who are continuing to hold a firm position excluding women from full participation in ministry roles.

However, I believe their position is going to get more and more difficult to maintain as the day we live in gets more and more perilous and more and more women are called and anointed by God, not to "fight for their rights" but to do exploits in the service of God.

It reminds me of a story someone once told regarding reconciliation. He said when the elevator you are on stops between the 26th floor and the 27th floor one night with you and a bunch of others and the light goes out and it's dark, nobody wants to know what color you are, what gender you are, whether you are rich or poor. They want to know, "Is anybody in here equipped to handle mechanics? Does anybody have a screwdriver?" You are not going to say, "Is there a black man in here with a screwdriver?" or "Is there a white man with an electronics degree?" You are going to say, "Is there anybody here who can help us?" It may be a woman with the screwdriver and a Vietnamese with the electronics degree.

Sometimes God puts us deliberately into a situation or a time that challenges us to find and accept one another's gifts, rather than one another's color, gender or class.

I think we are about to arrive at that time.

I believe Israel got to that time in Judges 4. Deborah was God's prophetess and she judged Israel. It was a fearful time in Israel, a bad time and no one worried about Deborah's gender. They needed help too badly. She, and she alone, according to the Bible, was able to stir up Barak, Israel's army commander, to rise up and throw off the yoke of Sisera and the Canaanite King Jabin.

Barak said to Deborah, "If thou wilt go with me, then I will go; but if thou wilt not go with me, then I will not go."

God is calling forth Deborahs in this endtime because the time is so evil, even for the Baraks who once thought they could do it alone. The Baraks who see and understand, together with the Deborahs, are going to bring about mighty victories in the last pages of Christian history.

I believe that a number of denominations are at this moment where Moses was in Numbers 27. The daughters of Zelophehad came to him to ask an equal inheritance for themselves in the Canaan distribution. Their father Zelophehad had died and left no sons.

Only sons could inherit their father's property and authority. Daughters had no rights at all. But these five courageous young women came before Moses and before Eleazar the priest and before all the congregation and asked for an equal possession among their father's kinsmen.

It was unheard of. It had never happened before. Moses didn't know how to answer them, but he did a very wise thing. He laid the matter, not before the priesthood, not before the congregation, but before the Lord. And God answered readily. God said, "The daughters of Zelophehad speak right. Thou shalt surely give them a possession of an inheritance among their father's brethren."

Moses obeyed God. And as a result of these daughters coming and asking for an equal inheritance and Moses and Joshua granting it, we find in Joshua 17, the daughters' tribe of Manasseh received ten extra portions of land allotted to them in Canaan. Can we expect less today? The daughters are courageously asking. Those who grant them their full inheritance will be greatly enriched themselves, their conquests for God greatly multiplied.

Nowhere else is this more clearly seen than in the Assemblies of God worldwide, now numbering 30,000,000. One secret of this growth is that "daughters" have been given an equal inheritance among the brethren.

One example of this within the Assemblies is our largest and fastest-growing assembly, Dr. Paul Yonggi Cho's church in South Korea, which now numbers some 700,000 adherents. It is divided into hundreds of cell churches, the majority of which, we are told, are pastored by women.

In closing, I would like to quote from the conclusion of the official statement on the Role of Women in Ministry that was adopted by the General Presbytery of the Assemblies of God, August 14-16, 1990:

> After examining the various translations and interpretations of biblical passages relating to the role of women in the first century church, and desiring to apply biblical principles to contemporary church practice, we conclude that we cannot find convincing evidence that the ministry of women is restricted according to some sacred or immutable principle.
>
> We are aware that the ministry and leadership of women are not accepted by some individuals both within and outside the Christian community. We condemn all prejudice and self promotion, by men or women. The existence in the secular world of bigotry against women cannot be denied. But there is no place

for such an attitude in the body of Christ. We acknowledge that attitudes of secular society, based on long-standing practice and tradition, have influenced the application of biblical principles to local circumstances. We desire wisely to respect yet help redeem cultures which are at variance with Kingdom principles.

Like Paul, we affirm that the Great Commission takes priority over every other consideration. We must reach men and women for Christ, no matter what their cultural or ethnic customs may be. The message of redemption has been carried to remote parts of the world through the ministry of dedicated, Spirit-filled men *and* women. A believer's gifts and anointing should still today make a way for his or her ministry. The Pentecostal ministry is not a profession to which men or women merely aspire; it must always be a divine calling, confirmed by the Spirit with a special gifting.

The Assemblies of God has been blessed and must continue to be blessed by the ministry of God's gifted and commissioned daughters. To the degree that we are convinced of our Pentecostal distinctives – that it is God who divinely calls and supernaturally anoints for ministry – we must continue to be open to the full use of women's gifts in ministry and spiritual leadership.[1]

NOTES

1. *The Role of Women in Ministry.* Springfield, MO: Gospel Publishing, 1990, p.12.

6

Silver's Legacy

Rev. Debra A. S. Quilling

When I think of her, which is often, considering she's been gone over 27 years now, I think first of her hands. Large, pioneer hands, the hands of a woman created to be strong and courageous. I think first of her hard-working, tender, story-telling hands.

Then, as memories begin flowing, I remember her voice, a prophet's voice – certain, convicted, words of wisdom, guidance and love in every sentence. I remember her poetry, her stories of homesteading in Montana, a place, a land still my home, the home of my father and my mother, of my cousins, the place I most experienced "belonging," even after having lived eighteen years in South Carolina. When they ask me of my home – it is Montana I remember and it is my grandmother, Silver, I see with the eyes of my heart.

Silver Tubbs Quilling Dobbs, my grandmother, my friend, my mentor, was a woman of deep Christian faith who believed and by prayer helped me believe too that God can use anybody who is willing. Likely my earliest memory was of those big, strong hands pressing down on my head like a bishop – praying to the God she served, to use her little granddaughter. She prayed God would call me to preach, would make the doors open and the way straight. I was no more than four years old when grandma began praying so specifically about me. She taught about the Word of God as she recited the Scriptures from memory, as she told me endless stories of God's work in the lives of people she knew. She helped me trust in a God who really cares for me, hears my prayer and wants to bring all children home to a relationship of mutual love and service.

Grandma Silver planted seeds each time we were together. She encouraged my faith, answered my questions and steered me in my choice-making. Grandma's Nazarene background and early Methodist instruction included prohibitions against activities which might lead to decadence, sin or life out of God's will. Until her death on Christmas of my fifteenth year, I sought her guidance about many things. I did not ignore her or water down her messages to me, I sat at her knee daily and I trusted her love and wisdom.

Especially powerful in these early memories of my grandmother is the knowledge that her eyesight and hearing were extremely poor and she could no longer read without a powerful magnifying glass and could hear only certain voices at certain levels of volume and pitch. She had seen her share of pain and loss. My husband and I are presently working on publishing her handwritten book about pioneering in Montana. Through her writings, we have learned even more about her struggles and her unwavering faith in Jesus Christ.

I was raised in the Methodist (United Methodist) Church by parents who were faithful in their church involvement and in teaching values which reflected God's Word. My father had come up in the Nazarene tradition, never missing worship. Even on school nights he accompanied his mother, my Grandma Silver, to church. Now, this much of a good thing was hard on a young boy, especially one who loved sports like my dad did, and does. Yet, he is still a faithful, committed church member today, nearing his eightieth birthday. When parents ask me if "making their child come to church will push them away from God" I can't help but think of my own father. I suppose I even comfort myself in reference to our two sons, now thirteen and fifteen, children of not one but two preachers. As with my father's, (and my own) childhood, my husband and I do not entertain requests to miss worship. Today, they don't ask us to let them miss but instead they try to encourage their friends to meet them at church. This is quite phenomenal in our time, my experience tells me. My grandmother's prayers and the prayers of my children's grandparents are powerful.

I have always trusted in God's awareness of my needs and in the leading of God's hand in life and that prayer is a necessary, life-giving activity for a child of God. My grandma was a powerful woman of prayer and she prayed for each of her children, grandchildren, and great-grandchildren. I want readers to understand that it was no accident, this calling upon my life. I wrote previously that my grandmother died during the Christmas season of my fifteenth year; I was barely sixteen when I heard a clear calling from God.

I always enjoyed friends of various denominational Christian backgrounds. I invited them to my church and they invited me to events sponsored by their churches. One such event included my first exposure to the evangelist, the Reverend Billy Graham. The United Methodist Church of my childhood had changed much since the early days of circuit riders and frontier churches. My church was quite formal and our activities fairly predictable. I loved my church then and I love it now for its mixture of people and backgrounds, but I had never seen anything like the movie the Assembly of God sponsored at the town's only movie theater.

It was a Sunday, and I had been taught that it was dangerous enough for the soul to attend a movie on weekdays but never, never, were we to go near a movie theater on Sunday. To tell the truth, the Assembly of God is so much more conservative than our church in so many ways I still am surprised they opened that theater and encouraged the town's young people to come. We did come too, by the hundreds. Sidney, Montana was not exactly an entertainment capital at anytime, but Sundays were especially quiet.

There are many things hard for me to explain about God's calling and the invitation to relationship which I have heard all my life. The night I went to the steps below the screen in that theater, following a movie, I cannot remember, and a message from Billy Graham I only recall in my heart for its impact, I knew God had a purpose for my life. I was scared, like a little child of four again, as I felt hands pressed on my head and heard prayers prayed by those who waited at "the altar."

Besides the grandmother I heard preach only in her home or the homes of others as she talked about God's love, mercy and judgment on a daily basis, I had known only male preachers (ordained ministers of churches I attended). I locked up the calling in my heart for a little while to do some sorting through.

I was 21 when I headed to Yale Divinity School in New Haven, Connecticut. I had double majored in Music Education and something called "Christian Thought" as an undergraduate. While I found the philosophy and religion classes fascinating, I had placed most of my academic emphasis on courses preparing for teaching and music performance. My plans had included attending graduate school in music through the University of Southern California. I had scholarship and grant opportunities through USC and looked forward to living on the West Coast. But God's plans were not the same as mine. In April of my senior year I heard God's voice while walking across campus to my next class. I knew I would never go to USC and instead of attending class I walked to the office of one of my professors of "Christian Thought."

Dr. Dicken was a popular professor and rarely available for informal, unscheduled conversation, but this particular day he was not only in his office but seemingly waiting for me to walk through the door. I poured my heart out to him telling of my uncertainty about this calling, wondering if it was music ministry to which God was moving me. He listened patiently as I told him of my lack of funding. I had a variety of money-generating jobs since I was eleven years old, all those funds were now depleted as I neared college graduation. Finally he broke into my monologue saying, "Debra, you're not going to believe this, but I just opened a letter from Yale Divinity School. They are welcoming the Institute of Sacred Music this fall as part of their graduate program, it is heavily endowed and full scholarships are available for music majors who want to explore pastoral or music ministry in the local church. I think God's opened the door for you!"

I applied to only one seminary, and during my years at Yale God gave me a certainty about the direction of my calling. God also gave me a partner with whom to share a challenging life. I was ordained in June of 1975 as a deacon in the Yellowstone Conference of the United Methodist Church and was married to Richard E. Allen, Jr. of Greeleyville, South Carolina in August of 1975.

This vocation I accepted has offered seemingly endless opportunities for Biblical positioning throughout the years, primarily by persons I knew in a very limited way or not at all. I have learned to allow frustration to rage around me and, by God's grace, remain calm in the center and wait for God to help the individuals work things out within their own hearts. It was not until my twenty-year high school class reunion that I knew something of the general perception of friends with whom I'd grown up.

For some it has been surprising that I would choose the Church. The Church was unpopular, along with most institutions, among persons of my generation. We grew up during the Vietnam era and many equated the Church with government institutions which were perceived as robbing us of our friends and our youth with no good, just reason.

Others have made a point of expressing their belief that I could have "made it" musically or as an actor. Many were amazed that I gave up potential fame and wealth for a God they scarcely knew.

Still others, my closer friends, were not altogether surprised. We had grown up as youth in Lonsdale Methodist Church, we'd been in Sunday school and youth group together. They knew of God's importance in my life and of my willingness to give time visiting the town's Rest Home with the pastors of our church each Sunday afternoon. I was always willing to preach when the time came for youth leadership of worship. I served in leadership positions in our youth fellowship and loved designing the Easter morning Sunrise services, held five miles out of Sidney on a hilltop, before daylight. I encouraged other youth to participate in church activities and never missed Sunday mornings with God and with my friends. Those who love and know me best knew these things about me.

In college I worked hard with other students and the college chaplain, Bob Holmes, exploring contemporary forms of worship. On Sundays when we were not offering our unique worship to churches, I would cross the campus on foot to attend the nearest church. Many Sundays I would go alone to the same Presbyterian Church never seeing another person under forty in attendance. I would sometimes invite friends, sometimes they'd even come with me, but that time alone in worship was not a bad thing and I knew, even then, how much I needed quiet time with the God on whom I counted for guidance and strength.

When, in 1974, I sought the support of my local church for certification of candidacy, a license to preach and recommendation for ordination the people who had raised me, taught me and knew me as their own, were thrilled to affirm my calling from God and voted their support unanimously at Charge Conference. Now, I will acknowledge an important truth while yet praising God and thanking my childhood church for such enthusiastic support.

I was the very first person, on record, to accept God's call out of the Lonsdale Methodist congregation and it would have been most uncomfortable for anyone who might have voted against the church's recommendation. Also, it is the policy of our church's system not to send persons back to serve as pastor of their home congregation. I was being "sent out" and that was acceptable and fairly safe. In later years, I knew some were not altogether happy about or supportive of women in ordained ministry. I always thanked God for sparing me that realization until I was old enough, experienced enough and already scarred enough to let it not wound me as it might have previously.

College and seminary were times of joy and support. I was blessed to study with Henri Nouwen and many other gentle, deep people of God while a seminary student. I practiced a way of prayer that has aided my spiritual growth and confirmed my dependence upon God.

Serving the church while a student in Connecticut included Associate and youth-minister roles at Park Street Congregational Church in Bridgeport, where I worked with an inner-city, multi-racial, economically diverse youth group. I served with Battelle Chapel at Yale and designed worship for children and youth of Yale professors while also directing a community children's choir. I did my final project for the Institute of Sacred Music with the children and youth of Nichols United Methodist in Trumbull, Connecticut. Each of these opportunities had some resistance, but for the most part I was comfortable and my role was fine with most of the church people. Nothing I had experienced, seen, or done prepared me for Wallace, South Carolina.

Of all the people in my early life, the two most concerned about my calling, my vocational choice and my future were my parents. Amy and Walter Quilling are well loved, precious people who have an enormous role in my well-being as a Christian and as a woman. They modeled faithfulness and strength. I could write pages about their importance in my life and the life of my family. Both were business people who taught me the importance of kindness and honesty and "letting things roll off." They taught me not to take myself and my feelings too seriously. But these two dear people were scared for me. They were afraid that I was going much too far from home, to a place that would not understand me. They worried that I had chosen to serve as a pastor; they had hoped I would choose music ministry, a much less threatening role for a woman. Until Wallace, I did not fully understand their fears. Now, twenty years down the road, I do understand and I am amazed they didn't insist and resist more than they did. I know now that faithfulness and trust in God kept them quiet when they wanted to speak many, many times.

The resistance I encountered in 1977 as appointed pastor to the Marlboro Circuit, three churches surrounding Wallace, South Carolina, was a trial by fire for me, spiritually, emotionally, mentally and physically. Richard was assigned the Blenheim Charge, three churches outside of Bennettsville, South Carolina. We had between us six churches, two parsonages, three counties, two telephone area codes and reputations as "hippies" even before we arrived. Looking at it now, I imagine we were mighty scary to those folks. Yale graduates (up north is up north), long hair, Richard's beard, our different last names, my strange Scandinavian accent, Richard's educated Southern accent and my hot orange Pinto with a plug hanging out of the oil pan. Actually, I could go on and on about our strangeness to these unique people, who were in their own ways equally strange and scary to me. Those early days require a chapter of their own to describe. I will do my best to condense a life-changing experience for the overview needed in these writings.

I was young, *very* young when Richard and I arrived with our U-HAUL at the Marlboro Circuit parsonage. It was a Wednesday and I had a prayer meeting at Pleasant Hill UMC that very night. I don't recall any food or people waiting for us, though it's possible someone was there and my memory is overcome by the hardness of the time. I remember a note on the door – informing me of my need to be at the meeting that night with a less than welcoming concluding message, some might even say threatening.

Richard was excited to get to Blenheim so we unloaded "my stuff" and he drove the U-HAUL on to Blenheim. The Wallace parsonage was an experience in itself but most memorable was flushing the toilet that first night, after prayer meeting, (which more people attended than ever before, I was told) and having it back up and back up and back up until the bathroom, hallway, kitchen and bedroom were flooded. I was sitting in the middle of this mess, wet boxes everywhere, sopping up what I could with paper towels when my Pastor-Parish Relations Committee (PPRC) Chair arrived. One of the many dynamics of my time in Wallace was the late night arrivals of this man with whom I eventually had a showdown about my role in his life. A tremendous lesson learned, so many lessons learned. Today I would thank him for his concerns and assure him I would call if I needed his help, otherwise not to visit without calling me first.

Richard and I had visited with the Pastor-Parish Relations Committees of our six churches several months before and I knew that many, no, *most* of the church people were very unhappy about my coming to serve among them. I had received phone calls from Wallace church people while still in Connecticut inviting me to forego the long ride south, so I was not surprised by the lack of welcome. I also didn't really know the traditions surrounding a new pastor's arrival. I didn't even know there was supposed to be a honeymoon period which might last a year or even two.

In some ways I believe I have been blessed by the pattern of my acceptance as a pastor. In each of my appointments my acceptance by the people could only get better – there was nowhere to go but up, so I never had to deal with the crash after the good times. I learned to accept that I was unacceptable. I learned to love without needing so much to be loved myself. It was a great and important lesson for a young girl from Montana who had enjoyed people all her life and taken for granted she would be loved by them for the most part.

In Wallace I put away many of my educated ways, I learned to listen with my heart, I learned about pain, rejection and broken-ness. I learned what caused the Samaritan to stop along the road to Jericho. God taught me compassion and surrender to God's will. God taught me about discernment and wisdom, about choosing battles carefully and leaning on the everlasting arms.

I survived Wallace, they survived me too. Because of my experience "trying to be the best pastor they'd ever had," I learned whose ministry I was part of and that it mattered very little that everybody loved me. I have many rich learnings and memories from Wallace but my favorites are two quotes, one from Vance English, a patriarch of the community and member of Oak Grove UMC. Mr. English was mowing the church lawn the first day I drove into the parking lot of the Oak Grove Church. When he saw me he came to a stop, turned off the tractor and slowly dismounted; much like the older cowboys used to dismount their horses after riding the range all day in eastern Montana. He came to me with a kind smile, an extended hand and a twinkle in his eye. "Well," he said, "Preacher lady, I just want you to know one day you're going to make everybody in this community happy." I was thrilled to hear this and responded, "Do you really think so?" "Yes, oh yes, you'll make some of us happy by comin' and the rest of us happy by going. One day we'll all be happy. " He smiled, one of many smiles he'd give me, he was my friend and I still quote him on his wisdom.

The other quotation was a word of comfort at a particularly difficult time for me. My friend Leonard Sweatt, a front-pew member of Pleasant Hill UMC, a man who had sorrow upon sorrow in his life yet still opened his heart to people and praised God for God's goodness. This dark day, Leonard gave me a hug and said "Just don't you worry about it now, God's looking out for you." I had come to Wallace just after the death of his only son, a teenage boy who died from diabetes. Len could barely walk for the crippling arthritis in his legs, he was a poor dirt farmer and had to work every day. His grandchildren, sons of his two daughters, had no daddies. Everybody lived in his little house with him. While serving as his pastor, I buried his beloved wife, Donnie, who died in the church during worship one Sunday morning. If Leonard Sweatt could believe God was looking out for him, so could I.

In addition to love and friendship and some strides in programming, two affirmations were great gifts to me from my Wallace days: (1) The people, after my first year, wanted me to stay and raised my salary so that I could, as an elder, be appointed to them again. (2) After my departure, they asked to have another woman assigned to their charge – although the Bishop and cabinet did not fulfill their request at that time, they presently do have a woman pastor serving there today, sixteen years later.

My other appointments in South Carolina included over four years in Myrtle Beach, a truly healing time for me. Both our sons were born while Richard was pastor of Socastee and I was associate minister at First UMC. My stories of this appointment are many. The funniest being the adjustment by my reluctant senior pastor to my existence as a woman clergy and as a pregnant associate pastor. Interestingly, it was the older people of the church who helped Tom most with flexibility in our work together. Tom got so open to the new style of ministry he would babysit my little boys in his office (I had a rolling crib/playpen) while I did counseling in my office. Talk about "coming a long way!" It was also striking how God prepares us for other new experiences. Tom's own daughter, Jan, is now an ordained, United Methodist minister raising children and working full-time in the local church. Tom and I are still good friends and it warms my heart when he credits our ministry together (and my existence) with his acceptance of God's call on his daughter's life.

I still enjoy visits to the church in Myrtle Beach. Their invitations to preach and sing are delightful to me. I will always be grateful for the years we had together.

I was called to campus ministry in 1983 and served for seven years as Campus Minister at the University of South Carolina. This was a major move for our family and painful as a clergy couple. Richard's church in Socastee had come through some major battles in transition from being a family-run country church to readiness to change and minister to the new population exploding in the once quiet Myrtle Beach and Socastee areas. As Socastee prepared to build and expand, we were moved to Columbia. This was a sacrifice for Richard, one of several he has made during our clergy couple marriage.

I loved campus ministry. It fit me well and I enjoyed the challenge of working with college-age people at major crossroads in their lives. One of the great gifts of my years in campus ministry was the opportunity to preach in churches all over the state. I had preached in hundreds of churches (there are over a thousand United Methodist churches in South Carolina). I had met appreciation sometimes, and also been shouted at and walked out on before worship, before preaching, just for being. These experiences were great preparation for one of the few United Methodist churches from whose pulpit I had never preached, my present appointment, Rehoboth UMC, Columbia.

I just began my sixth year as senior pastor at Rehoboth. Few would have foreseen my staying so long. Especially given the initial reception in June 1990. The church people were worried about this "woman preacher" they were being assigned and saw my appointment as a death knell for a congregation with several recent historical struggles. We are convinced now that God's will caused us to be together and have a wonderful vision for ministry developed over the last three years. We are entering a most exciting time in this church's history and are grateful. Rehoboth Church was once a country church with dirt roads, few people and almost no buildings in the area. Now this church named "Rehoboth" meaning "wide places in the city" (from the Biblical story of Jacob's search for a well) lives up to its prophetic name. In a heavily commercial area, the city has grown up around Rehoboth and we have tremendous opportunities for ministry to a very diverse community. The church is growing and the Holy Spirit is doing a great and wonderful work!

When my grandmother would talk with me about God's calling to men and women, boys and girls, she relied on scripture lessons like Joel 2:28-29, Galatians 3 :25-29, Matthew 21:15-16, Jeremiah 1:4-10, Mark 3:31-35, Mark 10:13-16, Luke 10:38-42, and my favorite, Matthew 19:37-40. I liked the Matthew passage especially, because I decided if God could use stones, God could use me.

I trust that God is the author of our lives and the finisher of the life and faith of the Church and that by God's will those called to serve will do so, the way will be cleared, strength will be provided and new days will come. I trust God's movement forward.

Faithful work, changing hearts, prayer and openness to God's spirit will continue the process toward God's intention for the Church. One day, not long from now, someone with just the right influence in a key moment of revelation will recognize God's message through the life of Jesus and accept that God's mercy and God's calling have no bounds. In the meantime, we pray for our sisters and brothers who find such possibilities for God's will impossible, and we work where we can for the healing and wholeness of Christ's beloved Church. May God keep us faithful and humble before the ministry being done through our lives and in Jesus' name.

7

The Evolution of a Call

Rev. Becky Brumfield-Stanley

One Christmas break during my early college years, my family traveled to the home of my grandmother in Lexington, Kentucky for the holidays. My grandmother's husband, Henry, whom we dearly loved, announced that he had been seriously considering my future. I was young and had given very little practical thought to life after college at the time. Henry had not only given thought, he had taken action. He had set up for me interviews with two women he felt could serve as role models for me in my future career. When the women arrived at the house, I was introduced to the wife of the senior and associate minister at my grandparent's church. When we were told of Henry's plans, they were surprised. I was as well.

Henry saw my gifts and abilities and knew my love of the church. The only way he knew for those talents to be used in the life of the church was in the traditional role of the minister's wife. When I later enrolled in seminary, Henry became my biggest supporter. He found a slide show on Women in the Ministry at Louisville Seminary and presented it at every occasion he could.

The church has always been an important part of my life. I was not aware of considering the ordained ministry as a vocation; although in many ways I have been preparing for it all my life. Winter Park Presbyterian Church, in which I was nurtured, had a staff of three full-time ministers, one retired Minister of Visitation, and a Director of Christian Education. As I was growing up, I assumed the only one of these roles available to me was that of educator. In the eighth grade I was assigned the task of reporting on a career. I spent time with Pat Williamson, our Director of Christian Education, and remember deciding that her job was not for me. I gave the assignment little thought after it was finished.

Throughout my teen years, the church was my second home. In our youth group, I found acceptance as an awkward teen and was challenged to relate my faith to everyday life. As part of a work camp in Webster County, West Virginia during my sophomore and junior years of high school, I was able to see a side of life that was not present in the affluent suburb of Orlando in which I lived. In the midst of poverty dirtying every hill and valley of that glorious landscape, I learned the value of hands-on charity. Youth from churches all over the country worked together to dig outhouses, build porches, tar roofs, paint, patch, and attach sheet rock.

The experience was unique – a local, ecumenical effort with the local priest doubling as plumbing contractor. The local people who translated the meaning of community of faith into concrete terms, sharing culture and tradition and building family ties. The work and witness of the Church had never been so real and meaningful for me! As I took one of my frequent breaks from the unfamiliar physical labor, I could feel the presence of God transforming my unskilled efforts into much needed shelter. Through that experience, the gospel became more than words or philosophy. It became a living, breathing reality calling me to give myself and allowing me to receive a lasting sense of purpose and direction.

In the summer of 1975, following my first work camp experience, I developed diabetes. The first few years of living with this were difficult, both emotionally and physically. Desperately trying to fit in and conform, I was painfully aware of anything which would brand me as different. At the same time, my body was reacting to illness and the usual stress of teenage existence in ways that brought me close to death several times. I remember being lifted up in prayer by groups within our church and others. This knowledge gave me a sense of connection and comfort while forcing me to trust in God's strength and rely upon my church family as well as my parents and sister.

The body of Christ was a true support for me and for my family in those trying years. I remember a deep comfort and trust in God's purposes and a surprising lack of fear, even in the most frightening of times.

These experiences gave to my faith a depth that added richness to the information I had received in youth meetings and confirmation class. The adults around me were able to provide guidance and connection between the feelings, frustrations, and fears I experienced and what I had been taught about God that enabled me to realize the possibility of a deep, personal relationship with God at an early age.

Having a sick child is a trying experience. Having an adolescent with a chronic disease provided a particular challenge for my parents. My second summer of work camp, when I insisted that I return, my mother signed up to go with me. Although this suggestion was for her peace of mind as well as to relieve the camp director of worry about my health, that work camp experience is one which continues to connect us to each other. My mother went as an additional adult supervisor, intending mostly to advise and protect. She ended up serving as work crew leader for a band of young people who were assigned work on a house owned by an older, failing couple. With God's help, she and that crew performed tasks that they knew nothing about before the two weeks of camp began! The following year, when I had gone on to college, she returned without me.

I spent my college years at Stetson University in Deland, Florida. Going away to school provided a wonderful opportunity to leave the cocoon of my home and church life and be exposed to the real world. I chose friends who were outside the safe realm of campus ministries and engaged in intellectual pursuits which challenged me to consider more of the world than my life until then had included. It was a constant effort for me to integrate my faith with my growing knowledge and experience. I had friends who had no religious background or training. I found myself in the role of apologist or even evangelist in communicating why it was that faith in God and Jesus Christ were important to me. The campus Christian community seemed sectarian and exclusive. In my newfound independence from the established church, I was forced to discover new ways of interpreting the faith, which was so personally meaningful to me, to those who did not know the language of the church. One friend declared herself an agnostic and shared how the deaths of her parents had left her questioning the existence of a loving God. Another had come from a family tradition of denying their Jewish heritage and struggled with very real moral dilemmas with little moral framework to rely upon. Because I attended a small, Baptist school, I found among my crowd many who were rebelling against strict interpretations of a "Thou shalt not" God. I saw these experiences as an opportunity to find my own way and separate the essential nature of my beliefs from their religious context. Although I grew in the personal ownership of my Christian faith and in my relationship to God, I was lonely for Christian community.

When I graduated from Stetson with a B.A. in Sociology in the spring of 1980, I realized that I had done little work to prepare me to succeed in the working world. I left with skills in counseling from work in the residence hall and a love of programming from working on the Student Activities Board, but no plan as to how to incorporate these skills into a paying job. I knew that I wanted to work with people. I had indications that I would like to do these in the context of a church situation. I discovered that the Presbyterian School of Christian Education in Richmond, Virginia had a dual-degree program, offering a Master of Arts in Christian Education and a Masters of Social Work from Virginia Commonwealth University. I enrolled.

I did not seriously consider becoming a Minister of the Word and Sacrament even after transferring to Union Theological Seminary in Richmond the following year. I thought that I might counsel or work in a church-related agency. I did know that the theology and Bible classes were fascinating and that I hungered for the Pastoral Care offerings which helped provide the context for these more learned disciplines in the real lives of people. I am not sure that it is because I am female that I was hesitant about my call. I feel that in every way my call has been uniquely personal and not political. However, I do know that I had no female role models until I came to the seminary campus and that meeting these extraordinary women made it more clear to me that there were those who combined the roles of minister and being female quite well.

The Presbyterian system required that I have some work experience in a local congregation before seeking ordination. It was not until I was faced with this requirement that I took seriously the call that God had extended to the ordained ministry. I did a year-long internship in Harrisonburg, Virginia, still purposely choosing a nontraditional role, that of beginning a Presbyterian Campus Ministry on the campus of James Madison University, rather than a more traditional church setting. Once I arrived, however, I found many opportunities for service in the life and work of First Presbyterian Church of Harrisonburg. I was involved in leading worship, teaching adult classes, advising the youth programs and children's ministries.

That loving congregation and my colleagues in ministry there gave me the chance to get my feet wet and discover how it felt to be the minister. There were opportunities to try new things, starting a young adults group and having Vacation Church School at night. The response was enthusiastic and the people were warm. The senior

pastor was a large man and a fatherly figure for the entire congregation. I remember one Sunday morning after assisting with worship
when a congregation member remarked to him, "How nice it is that
your daughter can join you up front every now and then!" Because
of my relationship with my colleague, I took that remark as a
compliment.

Fortified with that experience I returned to campus for my
final year in the fall of 1984. The number of women students was
growing and in the ivory tower environment I felt accepted and
encouraged for future ministry. It was during that final year, however, that I felt a difference in the way men and women students
were received. Men, particularly married men, were more marketable
in the job field. Competition creeps into even the most pious of
environments and all of our trust in the Sovereignty of God could
not gloss over the very human nature of the search process. One
good friend remembers the pride he felt and tried to hide when he
received a call to a church where our other friends had also interviewed. It was not until many years later that one of the others who
was considered shared that his rejection had been due to the fact that
he looked too young and that the successful candidate had been
prematurely gray.

I was determined not to be seen as a poor and pitiful typical
woman student who could not get a job. I took one of the first calls
offered and eagerly and naively jumped into the last Assistant Pastor
position in our denomination. (The Presbyterian Church USA abolished the position during their General Assembly 1995.) It was with
mixed emotions that I resigned that position a mere six weeks into
the job. The local Presbytery authorities had advised not to take this
position in which the Senior Minister had so much control; but I
advised them that I could look after myself. It took me six long
weeks to realize what was obvious to everyone else. Hiring a woman
assistant was a political feather in this man's cap. He was, as those
who knew him had advised me, not interested in what we could or
would do together, but in how he could work through me, a young
and naive female.

My naiveté was precisely what made this experience so difficult
for me. I had innocently assumed that I would succeed. I had ignored
the well-intentioned advice of others. My own disillusionment with
a church in which my ideas would be ignored and my sermons
rewritten was paralyzing. My healing came through the support and

love of friends, family, my future husband Mark, and an experience in the mountains of West Virginia.

A wise friend offered me the opportunity to supply three small churches for the winter of 1986. During that brief few months I preached three sermons a week, traveled icy roads in an old car, and experienced in a renewed way the call to minister to God's people in a local church.

My call began, no doubt, when I was a child experiencing in the church a sense of "home." It continued when, as a teenager, I eagerly awaited and befriended each summer intern from seminary. One of those interns had introduced to me the idea of attending the Presbyterian School of Christian Education in the first place. I did not discern the reality of my call, however, until I had tried it out for myself. My call is still not fully developed and my understanding of what it means for me to be a minister is in process every day. I am convinced that being a woman provides room for some flexibility within an often narrowly conceived perception of minister. I am also quite certain that it will always be difficult for me to fit who I truly have been created and called to be into that existing model.

The ways in which I carry out my call seem, at times, to go against the established grain. Although the more feminine characteristics of caring, nurturing, and service are what are admired in a man who chooses to give his life in service to the church, I am continually encouraged to be more assertive and to protect myself. During my first yearly evaluation when I served as Associate Minister in Charlotte, North Carolina, I remember being told that since I arrived there was renewed energy and excitement for the educational programs of the church. Immediately after that comment, I was admonished to "exert more leadership." The style of behind-the-scenes enabling was not what they were used to and because of that, the committee was convinced that I was not involved as leader.

I was ordained to the ministry in the fall of 1986 at the Albemarle Road Presbyterian Church in Charlotte, North Carolina. The service was very moving and I vividly remember the promises I made that day to serve God and that congregation. A few short months later, on that Christmas Eve, I became engaged to Mark Stanley, who was in the midst of an intern year from seminary. I remember being struck by the number of people who, after learning of my engagement and congratulating me, followed up with, "When will you be leaving us?" Several women added, "My call as a wife and mother has been the most rewarding part of my life."

The negation of my call as pastor over and against the other "calls" I have responded to has been an experience I have witnessed time and time again. This is not a unique experience. Because they often involve the resettling of two careers, the calls of married women are complicated. "What will your husband do?" is always the first question of an interviewing committee. The image and role of mother is a naturally positive one for me. Throughout my ordained ministry I have been pregnant three times and have juggled the roles of a working mother and professional minister for the majority of those years. The Biblical themes of expectancy and waiting have been graphically illustrated when I have been preaching during the season of Advent as a pregnant woman.

After losing our first son to a tragic accident in infancy, I know first-hand the pain of loss and can attest to the truth of Isaiah's comparison of God to "a nursing mother who cannot forget her child."

I learn from my two daughters and Mark and I share the anguish of other struggling parents each and every day. For me this provides many "homiletical leaps" through which the words of Scripture become words for today. Recently, I was preaching during Lent, focusing on our natural desire to skip past the unpleasantness of Jesus' suffering. I used the example of our daughter Elizabeth, who when watching movies on video tape always wants to fast-forward past the scary parts. The Good News of the Gospel is that even in the midst of those scary times, God is there to hold our hand. And God, our Heavenly Parent, does not keep us from the pain and hurt of life, but rather is there, holding us close, as we go through it.

Yet for many, my role as mother has been difficult to match with their picture of a professional. My preaching and teaching style are relational and personal. I think sometimes that I must be too approachable, too real, for some to feel comfortable. When Mark takes the children with him to some church event, he is praised for being "a family man." When I do the same, I am told that having them there distracts me from my job. I definitely find it difficult to carry the professional mantle of tradition, and authority comes only from the ability God has to work through me.

My favorite stories of my experience in the ministry come from the time when my husband and I served two small churches in Goochland County, Virginia. Mark was finishing seminary the first of our three years there and although I was technically the only minister, I was and remained "the minister's wife" for many until we left. This had its advantages.

One day I was visiting one of my friends who was a church member. She was the mother of three small girls and we were in the kitchen while she folded laundry. Her youngest, Samantha, came into the room and I picked her up and changed her diaper. When Teresa asked, "Is this a pastoral visit?" I replied, "I suppose so" which caused her to reflect that in the past, a visit from the minister had been an event to remember. The children were to be on their best behavior and the house spotless. "I cannot imagine ever telling a minister before you the things I've shared," she said.

The other of those small churches had mostly older members and few, if any, children. The ladies would take turns keeping my infant daughter in the nursery; but it made them uncomfortable for her to cry. One Sunday morning, following the Pastoral Prayer and before the sermon, I looked up from prayer to be handed Elizabeth, fresh from her morning nap. I sent someone to the car for her backpack and preached with her peeking out from over my shoulder. To this day when we see members of that congregation they tell that story!

I strongly believe that everyone is called to serve and given gifts which uniquely enable them to carry out their calling. Men and women who are called to the professional ministry each come as individuals with unique gifts, talents, and personalities. I have learned much from listening to the stories of others who have sought to be faithful in response to their particular calling. I do not know how to respond to the questions concerning the role of other denominations in ordaining women. You cannot force a congregation or another person to accept you as their pastor. We can only serve God faithfully and offer care, comfort, and guidance. God can and does use many methods for speaking to us – male ministers, female ministers, music, art, and literature are only a few of the ways.

I enjoy being the first female minister that persons meet. When I have that advantage I do not need to repair or correct or live in the laurels of the previous one. No male ministers have that luxury.

Women can and do bring a variety of gifts to the ministry. These gifts and women in service have traditionally been respected and honored by the church community. The ordination issue seems to be an issue of justice. Justice is never a clear and clean issue. Just because the higher governing body decrees that women *must* be ordained, that does not necessarily mean that individual churches *must* accept these women (or individual men) as pastor. Women must continue to respond to the call of God and the human institution of the church must continue to support *all* individuals in their calls. My denomination often is slow to support individual women, to take realistic steps to ensure their job placement or security. For us, the call of a pastor *must* be a two-way call, affirmed not only by the individual but by a church or position willing to accept her or him as pastor. I believe that the more experience church people have with women in the ministry, the more willing they will be to hear God speak to them in this way. The role of the higher governing body is to be beyond the personal prejudices and stereotypes that individual churches may have, to encourage congregations to take the risk, and to provide women with the opportunities to serve as God has called them.

8

Muriel's Response

Rev. Janet Vincent-Scaringe

Following the blessing and dismissal, Muriel picked up her cane and made her way to the narthex of the church. There she waited in line to greet the Rector of the parish. I was standing a few yards away by another door as I listened to Muriel's reaction to my first Sunday as St. John's seminarian assistant. I had already seen her reaction at communion as Muriel, lame as she was, made her way to the far altar rail – the rail at which I was not the chalice bearer. But, now at the rear of the church, as she tapped her cane against the stone floor of the revolutionary war era church, she exclaimed in a loud voice, "When can I expect to see her dressed in a 'dog collar'? I'm only glad that my dear brother didn't live to see this day!" With that, she turned her back to me and left the church for the short ride home. Muriel's brother had been a priest of the Episcopal Church and had died at a young age. She and her home-bound sister, both in retirement, lived in their family home and kept alive the memories of their dear brother and the church he had faithfully served.

It remained much the same for most of the Fall. Muriel would avoid my side of the rail each Sunday and reserve a few choice words for the Rector as she made her way out the door. By November, however, she began to acknowledge my presence with a nod of her head and the invectives so harshly uttered weeks before gave way to a simple "good morning." Just after Thanksgiving I received an invitation to have tea with Muriel and her sister.

I immediately went to the Rector seeking advice on what to do. He stared at the invitation as if it held some hidden meaning and after a long pause asked if I had ever seen the movie *Arsenic and Old Lace.* I had. As I drove to their home on the appointed day I was prepared to decline any cup of tea not prepared and poured in my presence!

What happened upon my arrival has stayed with me for the past fifteen years.

Muriel greeted me at the door and immediately led me in to meet Elsie. We were all a little nervous but they graciously told me stories of their home and family and showed me photographs of their brother. After tea (Yes, I did watch them sip before I did!), Muriel invited me to go upstairs with her to see her bedroom. She specifically wanted me to see the corner of her room which was her prayer place. As she slowly made her way up the flight of stairs Muriel described her habit of rising early each day for morning prayer and an extensive period of intercessions. I stood in the doorway and saw the chair and kneeling desk which she would use each day. On top of the desk was a notebook which contained a long list of people and situations she would pray for. Each had a date in the margin to indicate when Muriel had begun a new intercession. I had deliberately stayed in the doorway thinking her room too private a place for me to enter. But she invited me in with a wave of her hand and I knew that she wanted me to look at her notebook. And so I did. There toward the top of the page that Muriel had turned to, with the date September 15 in the margin, I saw my name. She had prayed for me from the first day of my arrival. There, in her room, I knew that I would be accepted as a presbyter in the Episcopal Church. I was a big problem for Muriel when I arrived at St. John's. But problem or not she knew that she was going to make room for me. Not because she thought women priests were a great idea or because I had impressed her as an individual. Muriel eventually made room for me because Grace had created a space within her where I could be accepted as a sister Christian and not as a threat to the Church she cherished. It was the same Grace which empowered me to put myself forward as a candidate for Holy Orders. We came to recognize that Grace in each other and nowadays Muriel allows as how she can't imagine the church without the ordained ministry of women as bishops, priests and deacons.

In the twelve years of my ordained ministry I have used this story as an illustration of the parable of the "Prodigal Son." You'll remember that at the end of the parable the younger (or prodigal) son is inside enjoying the feast given in his honor while the loving father is just outside the door of the home pleading with the older son to come in and rejoice over the good fortune of his brother. The parable ends with the father pleading and the son refusing, but the door is open and he may yet come in. In my sermons I point out that as much as we identify with the younger child's need to repent and return we are also the elder – often begrudging of God's mercy freely offered. We are all invited to the great banquet of God's salvation in Christ. We are created to rejoice not only in our own great fortune but also in each other's. I have not used this parable, also called "The Father's Love," or my story about Muriel as a vehicle to promote the ordination of women, but there is a message for those who would keep us outside the altar rail: We have already been welcomed into the great banquet – Jew and Greek, male and female, slave and free. In our communities all who have been welcomed into the meal have been made worthy of presiding at it. The decision as to who will preside and pastor has to do with gifts and not gender. Those who say otherwise have perhaps unwittingly placed themselves outside the door of the banquet and need to be coaxed back in.

As a child, my experiences of church came from the last years of pre-Vatican II Roman Catholicism. I was drawn to the mystery and beauty of the Latin Mass and would find myself day-dreaming that I was a priest. I never told anyone of my day-dreams as I knew that girls were supposed to be imagining themselves as nuns. I liked the nuns who taught me in grammar school and I watched them and others struggle with the changes wrought by Vatican II. "The ordinary of the Mass can be translated into English but the canon never will be," they said. Of course, the canon was translated and we were taught that the Eucharistic prayer did not have to be in Latin to be valid after all. As I grew older it would occur to me from time to time that I was drawn to the priesthood but each time I dismissed the notion as a fantasy.

I was drawn into the life of the Church. I witnessed first hand the extraordinary ministries of courageous men and women in the civil rights and anti-war movements of the 1960s. The local Roman Catholic and Episcopal parishes worked together on many programs and the leaders of both joined in hiding the Berrigan brothers during their time underground. As I grew into my teen and young adult years I understood that the people of God were not just to make sure that their souls were saved – they were to be a blessing to the world. By the time I was seventeen I knew that I would throw in my lot with the Episcopalians and for what seemed at the time an anti-clerical reason. I had read that Episcopal priests were not re-quired to celebrate the Eucharist every day whether or not there was a congregation. Indeed, they were only to preside at the Eucharist when at least one other person was present. The Eucharist was the great thanksgiving of the gathered community, not a ritual requirement of a few special people. I had done some reading in the Patristic era of Christianity and knew that the earliest church seemed to regard each baptized member as a co-celebrant. I wanted to be in a catholic denomination with that self-understanding even though I knew that there were many Episcopal lay people and clergy who would not have understood it quite that way. The Episcopal church seemed to invite discourse and ordinary people were allowed to join in.

While I became active in the Episcopal church, ordination was not in the forefront of my consciousness. I expected my work to be professional photography combined with active participation in my church and local community. I was interested in and supportive of the movement to ordain women in the Episcopal church but I wasn't sure that I actually had the gifts for priesthood. In the Fall of 1975 I went with a friend to attend a preaching mission conducted by a 75 year old Anglican Franciscan friar. During that mission I began a friendship with Brother David which caused me to reconsider my vocational choice. David discerned within me the gifts for priesthood which I was feeling tentative about. After all, I had chosen photography where my work was to stay behind the scenes photographing the action as it happened. An introvert by nature, I didn't know if I really could preach, teach and preside effectively. I also valued my privacy and from what I could see of the parish priest's life, it was all too public. David spoke to me of generosity and trust and I realized that a flame was being rekindled from many years before. He became my spiritual director and while the focus of the direction was on my deepening relationship with God, the question of vocation to the ordained ministry would raise itself as an invitation that I was being asked to consider. I was encouraged in this by members of my parish and after several years of struggling with the question knew that I did not only feel called to be a priest but wanted to be one as well.

In 1978 I was married to Carl Scaringe who was fully supportive of my decision to seek ordination. In 1979 I entered the diocesan process for those seeking ordination. The question itself had been decided by our General Convention in 1976 and the Diocese of New York had several women priests by the time I entered The General Theological Seminary in 1980. The "process" as we call it went fairly smoothly for me. The people on our diocesan Commission on Ministry, (the screening body which made recommendations to the bishop), were open to the ordination of women although I had several women friends in their late forties or early fifties who sometimes had a rough time of it. Some interviewers would ask if they were bored and looking for something to do now that their children were grown and out of the house. Sometimes that's a good question to ask men and women of a certain age who seem to be navigating without a rudder. But as a routine question for middle aged women with children it was eventually dropped. And none too soon.

My extended family and friends were in a bit of shock over my decision. No one really opposed it as much as they were confused as to what it would mean. I lost some friends who thought that my decision to offer myself for ordination made some sort of judgment on their lives and choices. It wasn't. But I soon realized that I now bore the projections of many childhood experiences of God and church and family. Not all of which were good. My husband's paternal grandmother spent the better part of an hour telling me that I ought to have my head examined while several friends, seeming to read her mind, sent business cards of good psychiatrists in New York City. Of course, there were those who were very affirming of my decision or came to be. Shortly after my ordination to the diaconate "Nana," as Carl's grandmother was called, gave him a one hour lecture on the importance of supporting me by his presence in church even on those Sunday mornings when his pillow seemed to be wrestling for his mid-morning attention!

As I reflect on it now, I think the sometimes muted support had to do with the fact that my family and friends had never seen a woman function as a priest. It was hard for them to imagine what my life would be like. What is a woman priest like? How does she dress? How does she hold and convey authority? They also worried that I would face a lot of strife in a church that wasn't unanimously sure that it wanted ordained women in its midst. I had many of the same questions. I didn't know any ordained women and so over several weeks I visited parishes where women were serving as priests. I, too, wanted to see what they looked like. My first visit was to a parish on the upper West Side of New York City. Not only did a woman serve in that parish, she was also the Rector. As the Sunday liturgy unfolded I watched every move she made, studied every gesture and listened to every inflection in her voice. What I was most aware of, however, was the way in which the congregation was not making a study of the celebrant – they were celebrating with her.

The liturgy went along with all joining in at the appropriate places. The hymns were sung with enthusiasm and the focus of this gathering of Christian people was the worship of God. Christianity hadn't been re-created with the ordination of this woman. And so I began my first year at seminary with the experience of having seen what I was hoping to become for the Church – a priest who was a woman.

The General Theological Seminary, in New York City, is the oldest Episcopal seminary in the country. Founded in the early 1800s it was modeled after Magdalene College, Oxford. The halls of the magnificent refectory are lined with paintings depicting the great men of General's past and old photographs show rows of cassock clad young men making their way to classes and chapel. I found the most tangible evidence of her exclusively male history in the restrooms, however, as with the exception of the guest restroom in the front lobby, all others had urinals. The architects, here and in England, had not anticipated the arrival of women!

I received a solid education at General. It was said that a few of the faculty members were opposed to the ordination of women but I never experienced any bias on the part of my professors. The women who had attended and graduated from G.T.S. in the mid-'60s and the '70s had already blazed the trail which made it possible for women and men to study for the priesthood side by side.

In June of 1983, newly ordained to the transitional diaconate, I went to work as the assistant at Grace Church in Nyack, New York. My immediate predecessor had been a woman and although she had only stayed for eighteen months she had broken the ice. I was interviewed by the Rector and a small committee of lay people and upon my arrival was warmly received. In January of 1984 I was ordained to the priesthood at Grace Church, surrounded by parishioners, friends and family. Just before the ordination I was interviewed by a local newspaper reporter and was dumbfounded by his last question: "What will you do if the Episcopal Church decides, at a later date, to repeal the ordination of women?" It really hadn't occurred to me that some might consider the ordination of women an "experiment" which would later be revoked if necessary. But, of course, that reporter spoke for the anxiety of many. Would the Church be torn apart? Would women prove to be incompetent as priests?

I was dumbfounded in December of 1983 when the reporter asked his question but as I write this article in 1995 I am not at all concerned about being "repealed." Ordained women have been serving the Episcopal Church faithfully and well for over twenty years. Someone once asked me how I convince people that women should be ordained. The answer was that I never try to convince anyone. I simply do my job. I have never preached about the ordination of women. I do preach on the power of the Gospel Sunday after Sunday. I tell stories, relate personal experiences, explore the meaning of a scriptural passage and work to form a Christian community from the great themes of salvation and self-offering love which the lectionary provides us with week after week. People respond to what is authentic in me and not just to my gender. Gender is not irrelevant, however, as my preaching and pastoring comes through the filter of my experiences as a white female, living in the Northeast.

When a parish or an individual experiences the ministry of an ordained woman for the first time, there is novelty and curiosity. But after the first encounter the work or the offering goes on: sermons are prepared, the Eucharistic prayer is spoken over the community, absolution is pronounced, the sacrament brought to the sick, classes taught and Christians formed for ministry in the world. The Christian community continues because nothing essential has changed.

Newt was a man in his early seventies when I met him in 1984. He had suffered a stroke and was paralyzed on one side and unable to speak except to mutter over and over again the syllables di da di da di. and occasionally "oh shit." His son called the church office to ask that someone bring his father communion. It was my day to visit the hospital and so I took the call. The son was a little nervous that the "woman priest" was sent but, as we entered the room, Newt was alert and welcomed me with a broad smile. After his release from the hospital, Newt went to live with his son, just two blocks from the church. Every couple of weeks I would go by with my home communion kit and we would visit for thirty minutes and end our time together with anointing for healing and communion. Conversations were difficult as Newt could only respond with a nod of his head or the familiar di da di da di. But we managed to communicate about different topics including his beloved N.Y. Mets during the baseball season. One day as I was about give Newt communion I began to recite the "Lord's Prayer." To our great surprise, Newt began to recite it as well. Every word was clearly and completely spoken. Newt's son ran into the room, tears streaming down his care-weary face. Until he died, several years later, Newt was able to recite the "Lord's Prayer." Needless to say, his slow recitation of that most familiar prayer became the highlight of every visit as Newt recited from the deepest part of his being, demonstrating to all that the stroke had not cut him off from his life in Christ. It was my privilege to be his pastor as he experienced the joy of being in communion.

Over and over again I have given thanks for the opportunity to respond to the call to ordination and to live out that call with people like Newt and so many others. Presiding at Eucharist or at a funeral or wedding, hearing the confession of a penitent brother or sister, teaching a class for parents preparing to have children baptized, in low moments and during Easter highs I have experienced the validity of my call through my parishioners.

I spent five and a half years at Grace Church. During the last couple of years I was interviewed by six search committees looking for a new rector for their parish. In the Episcopal Church, when a rector (or pastor) leaves, the parish begins a search process which includes receiving a list of candidates from the bishop's office. The search committee of the parish then interviews the candidate in a process of mutual discernment after which the parish issues a "call" to the candidate whose gifts they think will serve the parish best. Twice I was on the "short" list of candidates (one of those times the only candidate), only to have the parish stop their process to ask for another list of names – preferably men. Both times the parishes were afraid of what it would mean to have a woman as its rector – Would the parish be divided? Would new people join? At that time, of the 200 parishes in the Diocese, two had women as their rectors. Calling a woman was perceived as new and risky business.

In 1988 St. John's took the risk and Carl and I moved to Kingston, New York where I have been the Rector of this medium-sized parish for almost seven years. Several members were upset about the call of a woman. One, unbeknownst to me, went right out to her local funeral home to make funeral directions, explicitly forbidding the presence of any "lady minister" at her funeral. At the time she was 95 years old. Although I visited her regularly and arranged for meals to be delivered and visits from parishioners, she never did change her funeral directions. When she died at the age of 102 a retired colleague took the funeral which was held at the graveside. Miss Scott just couldn't trust that I would have allowed this colleague to hold the funeral in church without my assistance. Her Anglican upbringing was most important to her and so it was a source of considerable pain for me that my presence at St. John's prevented her from coming back to the parish one last time. Happily for me the vast majority of parishioners were eager to welcome me to St. John's. Over the years parishioners have left the community to find jobs, others have died, but many new people have joined as well. On any given year we enroll about 50 children into our Sunday School program. For the children it's just normal to have a woman as rector. Several years ago a family with two young sons moved to Vermont. A few weeks after their move I had a letter from them describing their first visit to the local Episcopal Church. As the procession made its way up the aisle the youngest son saw that the priest was a man. Pulling on his mother's sleeve he exclaimed in a loud voice, "Mom, men can be priests too?" She was happy to tell him that, yes, men can be priests too!

In 1990 I became dean of the local clericus and assumed leadership roles within our diocesan Conference of Deans and on our Commission on Ministry. I served with other women and men, lay and ordained, in leadership positions within the diocese. Ordained and lay women serve on the Bishop's staff and in June of 1995 New York became the fourth diocese to elect a woman as bishop. With the election of these women as bishops the Episcopal Church has welcomed them into the fullness of ordained leadership and service. There are some parishes who will not receive them still but the change has happened and in the years ahead the Church will benefit from their ministry and sacrifice. In the Diocese of New York some twenty women are now in charge of congregations. The wealthiest and largest parishes have been much slower to call women as rectors but that is slowly changing across the country. We are not alone. The same has also been true for African American and Latino priests as they seek to offer their gifts to the Church. We move slowly into the reign of God.

Many people think that the movement for the ordination of women has its roots in the civil rights and feminist movements of the 1950s through the 1970s. Others would point to the largely unrecorded history of women's organizations in the U.S.A. that not only paved the way for missionary work in the east and on the great frontier but paid for it as well. Certainly the role of women in the Christian Church has changed dramatically in the last one hundred and fifty years. Some might think it to be a matter of justice or of rights that women should be ordained but the Christian scriptures say very little about the rights of individuals. When talking about humanity the first thing our scriptures tell us is that we are all made in the image of God. Our inherent dignity as human creatures derives from that fact.

Further, we know that to be a Christian is to become a member of the Body of Christ. Christian denominations all hold that membership in the Body of Christ comes through Baptism. We believe that Baptism calls from us a personal renunciation of evil and a personal acceptance of Jesus as our Lord and Savior. We are then called into common worship through which we are continually sanctified, a life of prayer, and a life of service. Baptism is the entry point into the Christian life and the source of all Christian ministry. The soup kitchen worker, the hospital visitor, the teacher of catechumens, the bishop, priest and deacon, the peacemaker all come from the pool of the baptized. Should a woman be ordained? We might better ask: Should a woman be baptized? For the decision to ordain was made with the decision to baptize.

We know that this question was debated by the early church. Should we continue to incorporate a household or family by baptizing the head of the household or the father? Or, should each individual go through the rite and trauma of baptism? It was eventually decided that each individual should know the power of dying and rising in Christ through baptism. Each individual should understand herself or himself to be a new creation in Christ. A creation where it is no longer possible to distinguish between Jew or Greek, slave or free, male or female. It was understood that each individual possessed gifts for ministry and service which the Church would use. It is within this theological framework that Christians offer their service according to their gifts – regardless of gender, race or economic status. All service is equally honorable in the Kingdom of God.

The Roman Catholic Church, the Orthodox Church, some who have left the Episcopal Church and others make their case against the ordination of women based on the maleness of Christ and on tradition. They worry that to tamper with Holy Orders in any way is to run the risk of rendering them invalid. They understand the ordination of women as a dramatic departure from tradition and an essential change to the ordained ministry. I believe the flaw in their argument is to hold Holy Orders higher than baptism. In the early church a catechumen or candidate for baptism was prepared over a three year period. After baptism additional formation took place to guide the newly baptized into the new life of Christ. The baptismal liturgy began with the Great Vigil of Easter. It lasted all night until dawn brought forth the celebration of baptism and the first Eucharist of Easter. After their baptisms the new Christians were bathed in fragrant oil and clothed in new white garments. Their long preparation in the tradition of the church was over. They were now Christians. Ordinations were lackluster events by comparison. The time of preparation was not very long as the real preparation had already taken place before baptism. When the Church was in need of a bishop, priest or deacon it looked within its membership and called out someone with the appropriate gifts. Their ministry to the Church was held as sacred and vital for the nourishing of Christians, leadership of the Church and as icons of servant ministry but they were not held as elevated above the rest. Now it takes at least three years to prepare a priest for ordination and in many parishes only a few weeks to prepare for baptism. Ordinations are still apt to be grand liturgical occasions while baptisms can still be scheduled for Saturday afternoon as a small family affair. By our actions, which would you say is more significant? It's no wonder that the Church today spends so much time and effort trying to empower the laity. We have spent centuries convincing them that they are quasi Christians. The real Christians – the ordained, are the ones who have the important ministry. What is true is that bishops and priests (ordained pastors) minister to the Church so that the Church – the people of God – will be nourished for ministry in the world. Our ministry as the Church is to be a blessing to the world.

An important part of my ministry has been to strengthen our understanding of the importance of baptism. We work to make baptismal preparation significant and baptism itself a clear choice – not just a family tradition. Each year we offer a six month program for adults who wish to reaffirm their baptismal covenant. They are invited into a process of formation through prayer, engagement with scripture, service and reflection on how they understand their lives as ministry.

Who should be ordained? Those with the appropriate gifts of leadership, self-understanding, articulation of the faith, and perseverance should be ordained as the Church has need of them. It does not matter whether they are male or female. It does matter that we honor the baptismal covenant and dedicate ourselves to being God's people in the world.

In 1837 Lydia Maria Childs, author and abolitionist, reflecting on the growing influence of women in the Protestant churches, found an apt parallel in an old fable: The Fable of the Sorcerer's Apprentice.

After watching his master turn a broom into a man capable of carrying water from a nearby river, the apprentice decided to lighten his work by using the same spell himself. At first he was delighted to see the bewitched object sprouting arms and legs to do his bidding – until he realized that he had forgotten how to turn it back into a broom. As tubs, floor and furniture overflowed with water, the terrified apprentice cried "Stop! Stop! Stop! We shall all be drowned if you don't stop!" Childs drew the lesson with a smile: "Thus it is with those who urged women to become missionaries, and form tract societies. They have changed the household utensil to a living, energetic being; and they have no spell to turn it into a broom again." (I learned this story from Professor Fredricka Thompsett Harris while she was at the General Theological Seminary.)

In allowing women to offer their ministries as ordained leaders and servants the Church takes one more step in entering the reign of God it is called upon to proclaim.